Killer Copywriting Revolution:

Master The Art Of Writing Copy That Sells (Two Book Bundle)

Copyright Notice

Disclaimer

Claim This Now

The Ultimate Guide to Make Money Onlines

Grab your chance to own this comprehensive two audiobook bundle by Max Lane, covering everything you need to know about how to make money online and passive income ideas.

Including:

- *Make Money Online: Twelve Proven Methods to Earn Passive Income and Work from Anywhere in the World*
- *The Fastlane to Make Money Online: How to Write a Book and Make Passive Income with Self Publishing, Audiobooks and More*

Do you want to learn how to make money online consistently? Without a lot of fuss, scams, or investing any money?

If so - you've come to the right place....

THE ULTIMATE GUIDE TO MAKE MONEY ONLINE

Build a Passive Income Fortune with Kindle Publishing, Amazon FBA, Affiliate Marketing, Dropshipping, YouTube, Udemy, Blogging, Shopify and much more

(TWO BOOK BUNDLE)

FREE! Report reveals our most popular article headlines for driving traffic and attracting readers!

Find Out More

Killer Copywriting,

How to Write Copy That Sells

Contents

INTRODUCTION

CHAPTER 1: THE BASICS

What is Copywriting?

Copywriting Then and Now

Importance of Copywriting

CHAPTER 2: THE BOOT CAMP

Creating a Persona

Features vs Benefits

The Power of Words

Compelling Calls to Action

CHAPTER 3: THE BIG GUNS

Scientifically-Proven Copywriting Formulas

The You Language

Coffee Talks

CHAPTER 4: THE BATTLEFIELD

Ads and Headlines that Stick

Emails that Make You Click

Product Descriptions that Sell

Website Copy that Converts

Landing Pages that Hit the Mark

Conclusion

INTRODUCTION

Welcome to Operation: Killer Copywriting.

Your mission, should you choose to accept it, is to create compelling content, and learn how to sell any product or service thrown your way through the power of words.

Consider this your secret weapon.

Armed with this e-book, you have three targets to command and conquer:
- Target 01: Discover the key elements of good copy.
- Target 02: Master the secrets of conversion-driven writing.
- Target 03: Apply best practices in real business scenarios and accomplish all the free drills and exercises.

Should you be caught producing boring, irrelevant, or worse – plagiarized content – we will disavow any knowledge of your actions or purchase of this e-book.

This copy will never self-destruct and will be embedded in your brain as the most awesome introduction you've ever read.

Good luck!

CHAPTER 1: THE BASICS

Before you jump in to slaying your first winning headline or ad copy, let's cover a few basics first. In this chapter, you'll understand the importance of developing effective copywriting skills, the goal of a good copy, and the mind-blowing role of a great copywriter.

In the next chapters, you'll discover the proven strategies and tactics of copywriting, and learn how to apply best practices to real business scenarios. Just trust the process, have fun along the way, and we'll have you killing it in no time!

But first...

What is Copywriting?

Simply put, copywriting is the process of using words to make things sell better. What does this mean exactly? Let's break it down, shall we?

- **The process** – Yes, first and foremost, copywriting is a process. Unfortunately, it isn't about jumping straight to the writing part and simply putting a few words together. You first need to understand the channel or medium you're writing for, identify your goal, and study your target audience. How you write and what you write will heavily depend on these three factors – Don't worry, we'll guide you through every step of the way.

- **Using words** – Carefully chosen words can trigger an emotional response and spark your desired reaction from your target audience. Your copy needs to move them – excite them, scare them, touch them, shock them, inspire them. It's about knowing the power of using the right words to convince people to take a specific action, which brings us to the next phrase...

- **To sell better** – The goal of your copy, as part of any marketing strategy, is to convert. How you structure your copy can greatly influence how your audience behaves, and your simple choice of words may instantly spell the difference between a loss and a sale. You'll learn more about the power of words in the coming chapter.

That said, copywriting, by nature, is the most profitable skill to learn. So, congratulations on this investment into your current and future endeavors – wise choice, indeed!

With conversion as your goal, does this mean that copywriting is limited to ads then? Absolutely not.

Copywriting Then and Now
Before the wonderful world of the web existed, businesses would simply put up shop, possibly put out an advertisement on TV, radio, print, or OOH, explore telemarketing if needed, and maybe even direct mail. All those collaterals required copywriting.

These days, if your business isn't searchable online, you practically don't exist. And with search engines and social media networks running the show, quality content remains to be king. If you have or are thinking of putting up a business today, these are some of the things you'd probably have to consider writing copy for:

- Your branding / tagline
- Website
- Social media profiles
- Social media updates
- Social media ads
- Google ads
- Banner ads
- Video scripts
- Email marketing or newsletter
- Splash pages or sales pages
- Blog posts
- Articles for content marketing
- Infographics
- Presentations
- Industry reports
- Posters
- Flyers
- Brochures
- Proposals
- Sales letters
- Press releases
- E-books (yes, that's why we're doing this)

And the list goes on...

The more content you produce, the more chances for conversion. Great news is, this provides many work opportunities for copywriters! There's simply great demand for content, and nearly every aspect of a business requires a copywriter. Even brand guidelines, terms and conditions, and manuals need the amazing skills of copywriters! Design may be the first thing to catch someone's attention – but it's good copy that keeps someone hooked, and moved to click, download, sign-up, inquire, call, or buy.

Importance of Copywriting

While effective copywriting is profitable for any business, it's important to note that essentially, the *skill* involved is mastering how to use the right words to elicit a certain action. It's about effective communication and the power of persuasion. Once you learn the right words to put together, and the most effective way to frame them, the application of this skill set is endless. It won't just be about selling *a product or service* better, but even selling your ideas, opinion, and *yourself* better.

Imagine the possibilities...
- Effectively sell your products and services to your customers and exceed your sales quota.
- Competently share your thoughts with your team, and have them follow your lead.
- Confidently present your ideas to your boss, and finally get that raise or promotion you've been gunning for.
- Boldly talk about your skills with your head hunter, and grab that opportunity you've been waiting for.
- Skillfully discuss your proposal with possible investors, and finally close that business deal.
- Expertly win an argument with your partner on whose fault it really is this time – Okay... Let's not push it.

Are you ready to be a Master Manipulator?

Now that we've discussed the *what's,* head over to the next chapter and we'll walk you through the exact *how's* of killer copywriting!

CHAPTER 2: THE BOOT CAMP

In the previous chapter, you were briefly introduced to the process involved even *before* you start writing. In this boot camp, you'll learn exactly how to create your content plan to keep you on track throughout your copywriting task at hand.

Start with the end in mind.

It's important to set a crystal-clear goal for yourself to give your ideas direction and keep your writing style focused. And while you may be itching to simply jump straight to writing mode, I promise you this extra step will set you up for success.

What's your plan of attack?

It all begins by asking yourself these four questions:
- Who are you talking to?
- What do you want them to *know* about your product or service?
- What do you want them to *feel* while they're reading your copy?
- What do you want them to *do* after they read your copy?

Creating a Persona

Answering the first question is easy. Who is your copy intended for? Male and female college students who may need help with certain subjects, stay at home moms searching for a convenient fitness app, or men in their 50s who want to try a new hobby? While identifying certain demographics as your target audience is often simple, creating a persona is even better.

What is a persona?

Building a user persona means going beyond just a collective age bracket, gender, or lifestyle. It's about putting a face to your target reader, stepping into their world, determining their challenges and pain points, finding out their dreams and aspirations, and spotting the opportunity of how your product or service can be what motivates them to reach their goals.

Who's the ideal person who would want your product or service? To develop a good understanding of your target customer, a little research can go a long way. Good news is, this "research" may actually be easier than you think – people are just more than willing to voice out their concerns and opinions about anything and everything these days. Just check your Facebook feed... See what I mean?

How to Get Started

It may feel a bit stalker-y at times, so best consider yourself as an undercover spy. Here are a few methods you may want to try:

- Check out social media groups and hashtags related to your topic – Those ### are dying to be clicked on! What's the general sentiment? What are people saying? What do they like and dislike about products similar to yours?
- Check out Amazon, Yelp, and other review sites that are relevant to your business. You can also browse through comments on related blog posts and videos. That's a market insight heaven right there. What are their common challenges? Which expectations were not met?
- Talk to people similar to your target audience (your Millennial niece maybe?), or better yet,

talk directly to your customers. If you already have an existing database, try reaching out for a survey or see if there are any patterns in your customers' questions and feedback.

By doing these and immersing yourself in their world, not only will you gain valuable market insights – You'll learn to use their language, too. Instead of using technical words or business jargon, you can echo their sentiments, expressions and tone in your copy. This will also help you gain their trust and respect, as they'd appreciate being spoken to in a manner they're most familiar and comfortable with.

Drill #1

Create your own persona for a new mobile phone that your client will launch next month. Here's a table you can fill out to help you get started:

Demographics	Age, gender, education, income, status?
Career Background	Industry, job, responsibility, career path?
Career Goals	More time, more income, more awards?
Personal Interests	What are their hobbies, where do they go often?
Attitude and Values	Are they health-conscious, eco-friendly, thrifty?
Challenges	What are their main frustrations?
Potential Bottlenecks	What could be their possible objections about using your product / service?

For the purpose of this exercise and the following drills throughout this e-book, here's our sample persona:

Samantha is a young professional in her early 20s. She's an associate for an events company and works directly with various clients and suppliers. She loves her job, and though it's a fast-paced industry, she finds herself still wanting to do more outside work – She needs another outlet for her creative, adventurous spirit. She's the first to try the latest trends, and post about them on her social media. Secretly, she's dying to be an IG-influencer and luckily, being in the events industry has helped her build the right connections for it. Being offline or having her phone die on her in the middle of the day is her worst nightmare – Imagine all the possible messages, calls, or IG-worthy moments she could be missing every minute she's disconnected.

By creating a persona, you can focus your research and dig deeper into your target customer's culture. The more you know about them, the better you can tailor your copy to speak directly to them. The most important points to identify are their main challenges and potential bottlenecks. Remember – your goal is to be *the* solution they've been waiting for.

Features vs Benefits

Now that you've studied your market, let's move on to the next question: What do you want them to know about your product or service? Instinctively, you might just start listing down your product features and how it's the first, the new, the best, the one, the only...

Features tell. Benefits sell.

Product features are important, they're what *literally* sets one product apart from another – Its specs, colors, materials, and so on. But it's translating these features into relevant benefits that will give your offer a competitive edge.

Instead of just listing and telling your customers all your amazing product features, it would be wiser (and a lot less boring) to sell the *results*. How will they benefit from your product? Go back to your persona and paint a picture of how your product's features will help them address their frustrations or achieve their goals.

Here's a cool trick to help you turn basic features into key benefits – Simply ask, *so what?*

Drill #2

So instead of saying...

> *This awesome new phone weighs only 157g, with 6.3" Quad HD+ Super AMOLED (2960 x 1440), 521 ppi infinity display. It's available in Black Pearl, Blue Coral, Black Onyx, Gold Platinum, Silver Titanium, White Pearl, and Pink Gold. It has a 4000MAh battery capacity, and comes with 128GB internal storage and 6GB RAM. Best of all, it has a Dual Camera with dual OIS – Wide-angle camera and Telephoto camera.*

Try breaking down the important features and ask yourself – so what?

- *This awesome new phone weighs only 157g*
  So what?
  It's perfect for your versatile, on-the-go and active lifestyle!

- *6.3" Quad HD+ Super AMOLED (2960 x 1440), 521 ppi infinity display*
  So what?
  You don't miss a single detail while watching and editing your videos!

- *It's available in Black Pearl, Blue Coral, Black Onyx, Gold Platinum, Silver Titanium, White Pearl, and Pink Gold*
  So what?
  You're sure to find one that perfectly suits your style!

- *It has a 4000MAh battery capacity*
  So what?
  Your phone can finally keep up with your demanding mobile lifestyle!

- *Comes with 128GB internal storage and 6GB RAM*
  So what?
  You can build and keep more memories – not delete them!

- *Best of all, it has a Dual Camera with dual OIS – Wide-angle camera and Telephoto camera.*
  So what?

You can capture perfect moments #forthegram all day and night!

Now you have a more interesting list of solutions to sell your persona. They can then go into the specs and further details if they're interested to know more.

The Power of Words

Words have the power to cut to the core and connect with you customers on a deep emotional level. They also hold the answer to the next question on your content plan – What do you want your customers to *feel*?

The Three Most Powerful Words
Discover.
Free.
Secret.

These are some of the most powerful words used in sales as they spark a certain emotion. They make you *feel* something – excited, intrigued, or curious at the very least.

After you identify your product benefits, keep asking *so what* until you dig into an emotional benefit. What does your customer *really* care about?

Persuasive copy harnesses the power of emotion to appeal to an inner craving. What are your persona's dreams and aspirations, what do they value most? Is it fame? Power? Prestige? Security? Health?

Once you've identified this, you can add more detail to your copy and paint a clear picture that evokes a genuine feeling.

Seven Saleable Emotions

To write an even more compelling copy, try working around the seven most effective emotions to trigger:

- *Fear* – This is definitely one of, if not, the most powerful emotion you can use to hook your reader. How many times have you agreed to do or buy something simply out of fear?

- *Encouragement* – We could always use a little encouragement, especially when we're already frustrated with whatever challenges we're facing. If a product filled with hope of solving your problem suddenly pops on your feed, wouldn't that catch your attention?
- *Anger* – While some people may appreciate encouraging copy, some may respond better to a product that echoes exactly what they're feeling. They're beyond disappointed, they're absolutely mad, and they need a solution NOW!!! (Hint: That's you.)

- *Curiosity / Secrecy* – The tease of a secret or something forbidden is just too hard to resist! Feed your customer's curiosity to get that click.

- *Safety / Security* – Selling, itself, isn't the biggest challenge – It's gaining trust. Present yourself as a trust-worthy business, and you've got one foot in the door.

- *Lust* – It's no secret, sex sells. And a good copywriter can make almost anything look and sound sexy!

- *Greed* – But wait, there's more! The promise of more money, more savings, the best, the highest, and the greatest are the most overused copy points, but simply because they're still extremely effective.

So, Master Manipulator, which of these buttons would you like to push? Here are a few power words you can use to boost your copy and achieve a compelling emotional impact!

Powerful Words that Trigger Fear

Agony	Backlash	Blood	Beware
Apocalypse	Beating	Blunder	Blinded
Armageddon	Bloodbath	Bloodcurdling	Bloody
Assault	Bomb	Buffoon	Bumbling
Cadaver	Catastrophe	Caution	Collapse
Catastrophe	Cripple	Crazy	Danger
Crisis	Deadly	Destroy	Deceiving
Death	Devastating	Disastrous	Embarrass
Dumb	Drowning	Doom	Fail
Feeble	Fired	Frantic	Fooled
Fool	Frightening	Gullible	Gambling
Hack	Hoax	Hazardous	Invasion
Holocaust	Hurricane	Insidious	Injure
Horrific	Lawsuit	Jail	Jeopardy
Lawsuit	Looming	Massacre	Lurking
Lunatic	Meltdown	Mistake	Mired
Menacing	Murder	Nightmare	Pale

Painful	Panic	Peril	Pitfall
Piranha	Plague	Plunge	Plummet
Played	Poison	Prison	Poor
Pummel	Risky	Reckoning	Revenge
Refugee	Pus	Searing	Scream
Scary	Silly	Shellacking	Slaughter
Shatter	Slave	Strangle	Stupid
Tailspin	Tank	Targeted	Teetering
Terror	Terrorist	Trap	Toxic
Tragedy	Torture	Volatile	Victim
Vaporize	Vulnerable	Wounded	Worry
Warning			

Powerful Words that Trigger Encouragement

Amazing	Ascend	Astonishing	Astounding
Audacious	Awe-inspiring	Awesome	Badass
Backbone	Blissful	Belief	Beat
Brilliant	Bravery	Breathtaking	Celebrate
Cheer	Command	Colossal	Conquer
Courage	Defiance	Defeat	Daring
Dominate	Delight	Dignity	Devoted
Effortless	Empower	Excited	Excellent
Epic	Extraordinary	Eye-opening	Fabulous
Faith	Fantastic	Fearless	Ferocious
Fierce	Force	Fulfill	Glorious
Glory	Graceful	Grateful	Grateful
Guts	Happy	Heart	Hero
Hope	Honor	Incredible	Jubilant
Jaw-dropping	Legend	Life-changing	Magic

Miraculous	Miracle	Mind-blowing	Master
Marvelous	Noble	Perfect	Persuade
Phenomenal	Pluck	Power-Up	Praise
Prevail	Remarkable	Revel	Rule
Sensational	Seize	Score	Spectacular
Splendid	Spirit	Spine	Spunk
Staggering	Strengthen	Striking	Supreme
Stunning	Stunt	Strong	Surprising
Terrific	Thrive	Thwart	Titan
Tough	Tremendous	Triumph	Unbeatable
Unbelievable	Unforgettable	Unique	Unleash
Uplifting	Valiant	Valor	Vanquish
Victory	Win	Wonderful	Wondrous

Powerful Words that Trigger Anger

Abhorrent	Arrogant	Ass-kicking	Abuse
Annoying	Bash	Barbaric	Backstabbing
Blatant	Big mouth	Beat-down	Brutal
Bullshit	Bully	Cocky	Coward
Clown	Cheat	Corrupt	Clobber
Curse	Crush	Crooked	Debase
Desecrate	Delinquent	Defile	Demolish
Disgusting	Dishonest	Disgusting	Evil
Exploit	Force-fed	Full of shit	Freaking out
Full of shit	Greedy	Gross	Harass
Horrid	High and mighty	Hate	Infuriating

Jackass	Kick	Kill	Knock Out
Knock	Know it all	Livid	Lies
Loathsome	Loser	Lying	Maul
Misleading	Money-grubbing	Nasty	No Good
Nazi	Obnoxious	Oppressive	Payback
Pain in the ass	Perverse	Pest	Pesky
Phony	Pissed off	Pompous	Pollute
Pound	Punch	Pretentious	Preposterous
Punish	Rampant	Repelling	Ravage
Revile	Repugnant	Revolting	Rude
Rotten	Ruined	Ruthless	Scam
Savage	Sick and tired	Scold	Slam
Sink	Slander	Slay	Slap
Smash	Smug	Smear	Sniveling
Snooty	Snob	Spoil	Snotty
Stuck up	Suck	Terrorize	Trounce
Trash	Up to here	Underhanded	Violate
Tyranny			

Powerful Words that Trigger Curiosity

Ancient	Backdoor	Banned	Behind the scenes
Black Market	Blacklisted	Bootleg	Censored
Classified	Cloak and dagger	Concealed	Confessions
Confidential	Controversial	Covert	Cover-up
Exotic	Forbidden	Forgotten	From the vault
Hidden	Hush-hush	Illegal	Insider

Little-known	Lost	Never seen before	Off the record
Off-limits	Outlawed	Private	Restricted
Sealed	Secret	Smuggled	Strange
Tried to hide	Unauthorize d	Uncensored	Under wraps
Undercover	Undergroun d	Under-the-table	Undisclosed
Unexpected	Unlock	Unreachable	Unspoken
Unveiled	Withheld		

Powerful Words that Trigger Safety

Above and beyond	Anonymous	Authentic	Automatic
Backed	Bankable	Best-selling	Clockwork
Certified	Cancel anytime	Endorsed	Foolproof
Ironclad	Lifetime	Guaranteed	Money-back
No-fail	No risk	No questions asked	No strings attached
No obligation	Official	Professional	Permanent
Protected	Privacy	Proven	Recession-proof
Reliable	Refund	Results	Research
Risk-free	Rock-solid	Science-backed	Survive
Secure	Sure-fire	Scientific	Tested
Trustworthy	That never fails	Thorough	Try before you buy
Uncondition al	World-class	Verify	

Powerful Words that Trigger Lust

	Allure	Arouse	Bare
Begging	Beguiling	Brazen	Captivating
Charm	Cheeky	Climax	Crave
Delight	Delirious	Depraved	Desire

Dirty	Divine	Ecstasy	Embrace
Enchant	Enthralling	Entice	Entrance
Excite	Explicit	Exposed	Fascinate
Forbidden	Frisky	Goosebumps	Hanker
Heavenly	Hottest	Hypnotic	Impure
Indecent	Intense	Intoxicating	Itching
Juicy	Kinky	Kiss	Lascivious
Lewd	Lick	Lonely	Longing
Love	Lure	Luscious	Lush
Lust	Mischievous	Mouth-watering	Naked
Naughty	Nude	Obscene	Orgasmic
Passionate	Pining	Pleasure	Provocative
Racy	Raunchy	Risqué	Rowdy
Salacious	Satisfy	Saucy	Scandalous
Seduce	Seductive	Sensual	Sex
Shameless	Sinful	Sleazy	Sleeping
Spank	Spellbinding	Spicy	Steamy
Stimulating	Strip	Sweaty	Tantalizing
Taste	Tawdry	Tease	Tempting
Thrilling	Tickle	Tight	Tingle
Turn on	Unabashed	Uncensored	Untamed
Untouched	Urge	Voluptuous	Vulgar
Wet	Whip	Wild	Yummy

Powerful Words that Trigger Greed

	Bank	Bargain	Best
Billion	Bonanza	Booked solid	Cash
Cheap	Costly	Discount	Dollar
Double	Explode	Extra	Feast
Fortune	Free	Freebie	Frenzy
Frugal	Gift	Golden	Greatest
High-paying	Inexpensive	Jackpot	Lowest price
Luxurious	Marked down	Massive	Money
Money-draining	Money-saving	Nest egg	Pay zero

Prize	Profit	Quadruple	Reduced
Rich	Savings	Six-figure	Skyrocket
Soaring	Surge	Treasure	Triple
Waste	Wealth	Whopping	

Drill #3

Now that you're equipped with power words, let's go back to your persona and our sample phone product benefits. This time, ask *so what* again, choose a value you want to address, and an emotion you'd like to trigger. Finally, draft an emotional benefit and amplify them with some power words!

Here's an example of the different ways you can sell the phone's *4000MAh battery capacity*. Complete the table with four more emotional benefits.

Product Benefit	Goals / Value	Emotion	Emotional Benefit
This phone can finally keep up with your demanding mobile lifestyle!	Connections, Time, Wants to be an IG Influencer	Fear	What if your phone fails you again when you need it most?
		Greed	Don't waste a single minute to build another connection.
		Encouragement	Make every day, epic.

Making your target audience feel something is key. The more you know about them, the better you can shape your copy to spark the right emotion.

And now that they're hooked, you can finally answer the last question – What do you want them to *do*?

Compelling Calls to Action

Now this last bit is often the simplest, but most overlooked part of a content plan. Sometimes, you may assume your reader should obviously click on your copy, and that you clearly want them to buy already – but do you really want to leave that to chance?

Your readers are bombarded with creative and exciting offers every day, and they may easily just look away for a second and click on something else. Simply adding that extra word, phrase or button may be all the reminder they need to close the deal. Keep your copy foolproof, and make conversion as easy and effortless as possible with a compelling call to action.

How to Write an Effective Call to Action (CTA)
While a simple "click here" or "call now" may do the trick, here are some other surefire ways to phrase your call to action. Explore different styles and see which works best for your product, service and offer.

- **Be direct** – Keep it short and simple. This is where your *click here* and *call now* would fall under, together with the *sign-up here* and *download now*. Absolutely nothing wrong with these! Sometimes, readers just need to know where to click.

- **Make it interesting** – You could also add the emotional benefit to make your CTA more appealing. There's always room to make your copy more creative, personal and relevant to your target audience. *Click here to start making every day epic*. Or *Call now for a brighter future, today.*

- **Use power words** – As covered in The Power of Words section earlier, these are scientifically-proven words that compel customers to action. These include *new, discover, free, act now*, and the extensive list from the previous chapter. If you combine power words with your emotional benefit, you could say *Click here and discover how you can make every day epic*.

- **Sound urgent** – Aside from adding *now* or *today* in your CTAs, you could also hint at having a limited time or a limited number of items for your offer. Adding phrases like *don't miss out* or *before it's all gone* should do the trick. Again, you could also be more creative and say *Sign-up now before someone steals your spot* or *Buy now while we still have this in your size!*

- **Remove the risks** – Gaining your target audience's trust can be challenging, especially if they're just hearing about your business for the first time. They may be really interested, and just need some form of assurance to help put their hesitation at bay. To make your CTA more appealing, you can throw in a risk-free clause with your offer. *Sign-up now for your free 30-day trial*. *Subscribe now and cancel anytime*. Phrases like *no credit card needed* and *full money back guarantee* are also all-time favorites for a reason. They simply work!

Try to write at least 10 creative calls to action that relate to your samples from Drill #3. Don't forget to explore different styles and combinations of power words!

Remember, the ultimate goal of any sales copy is conversion – and a compelling call to action is the last piece of the puzzle your readers need to complete their transaction.

Now jump to the next chapter to discover the secrets of killer copywriting, before others beat you to it!

CHAPTER 3: THE BIG GUNS

You've finally mapped out your plan of action. You've gained valuable insights about your persona, you've identified their pain points and how your product benefits are the answer, you've selected an emotion you believe they'll best connect with, and you have the right power words to trigger them to follow your clear call to action.

Now it's time to put all those key elements together, and start writing!

In this chapter, you'll finally get your hands dirty and learn the
the proven formulas, strategies and tactics of effective copywriting. So, gear up and get ready to take on the big guns. It's open season!

Scientifically-Proven Copywriting Formulas

Did you ever wish there was just a formula you could simply follow to produce effective copy? There is. There are quite a few, actually, and you're about to meet the two women on top – AIDA and PAS.

AIDA

AIDA has long been known to be the princess of copywriting. She's been in the business for so long – since the 1900s – that you should just consider her to be *the queen* of copywriting. She rules when it comes to presenting product benefits, in an interesting way.

AIDA stands for Attention, Interest, Desire, and Action, and here's how you can make her the star of your copy:

- **Attention** – Start with a bold headline. As an ancient queen, AIDA lives by the old saying, go big or go home. Start with a bang to immediately get your reader's attention, then teasingly lure them in to your lair.

- **Interest** – Now that you got your target's attention, present them with your product benefits. Why do they need your product, how can it solve their challenges? What's in it for them? Dangle these beauties in their faces. But that's not enough, remember that nagging question you need to ask yourself? *So what?*
- **Desire** – Now you need to dig deeper and hook them with your *emotional benefits*. They now know that they need you, but it's time to make them *want* you, too. Paint a picture of how your product can help them reach their dreams and aspirations. Present further proof or a bigger reason to buy in. This is the point that makes them go *I need this in my life now, just shut up and take my money!!!*
- **Action** – And finally, simply tell them what to do so they can finally take home the product or service of their dreams.

PAS

PAS, on the other hand, is the more mischievous of the two ladies. While AIDA focuses on your customers' dreams and aspirations, PAS thrives on their fears and nightmares. She's highly effective in her craft as more than wanting some good every now and then, people definitely want to avoid something bad at all cost!

PAS stands for Problem, Agitate, Solution, and this is how she operates:

- **Problem** – Open your proposal with a problem. What's your persona's biggest pain point? That will be your selling point. People will do anything to avoid any hassle, pain, or headache. So, remind them of their problem!

- **Agitate** – Next, amplify that problem. Add salt to the wound, and fuel to the fire. Use power words that trigger fear and anger. Make their frustrations larger than life and just before they lose it...
- **Solution** – Present yourself as the solution. Paint a picture of how much greener the grass is on your side, and how wonderful life can be if they only take that one last step to end their nightmare... Which is to finally close the deal with you.

Tricky, isn't she? But imagine how much more powerful your copy can be when these two ladies work together.

Drill #5

Here's an example of a landing page from Basecamp. Can you identify which formula they used?

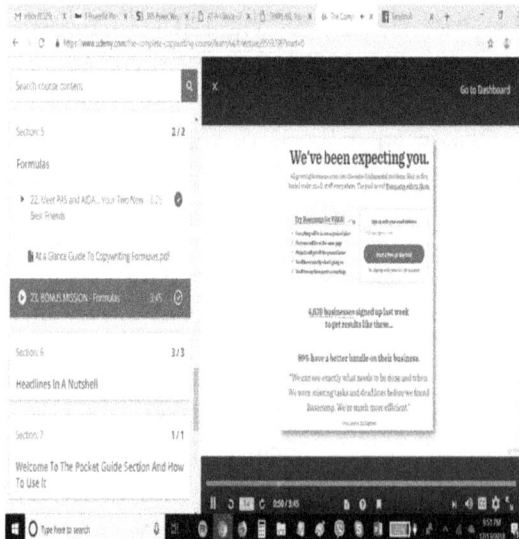

Yup, that was a trick question. This sample makes use of both formulas! So, as you can see, you can use them for anything from a headline, to an ad, an EDM, a splash page, and so on.

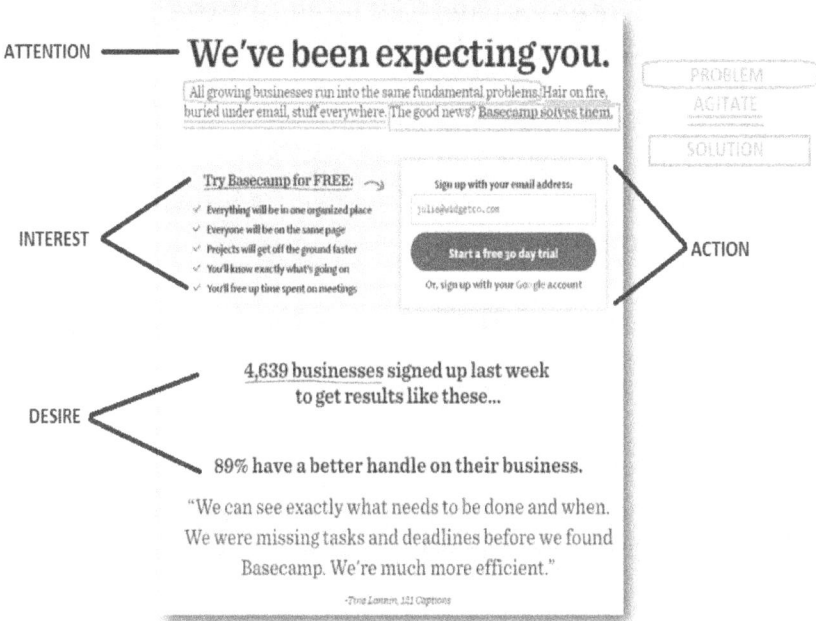

ATTENTION — **We've been expecting you.**

PROBLEM
AGITATE
SOLUTION

All growing businesses run into the same fundamental problems. Hair on fire, buried under email, stuff everywhere. The good news? Basecamp solves them.

Try Basecamp for FREE:

INTEREST
- Everything will be in one organized place
- Everyone will be on the same page
- Projects will get off the ground faster
- You'll know exactly what's going on
- You'll free up time spent on meetings

Sign up with your email address:

julie@widgetco.com

Start a free 30 day trial

Or, sign up with your Google account

ACTION

4,639 businesses signed up last week to get results like these...

DESIRE

89% have a better handle on their business.

"We can see exactly what needs to be done and when. We were missing tasks and deadlines before we found Basecamp. We're much more efficient."

-Tina Larson, 121 Captions

Who run the world? These girls certainly, do. And while there are many other formulas out there, they're mostly just variations of AIDA and PAS.

Try creating sample copies for the same mobile phone in the previous exercises. Write one sample using the AIDA formula, one sample using the PAS formula, and one sample combining both!

What's important for you to remember is that formulas are fluid and flexible. They're just basic principles of how you can shape or layout your copy – But what you say, is still more important than how you say it.

You can have the boldest headline, sell the most appealing benefits, or highlight the most frustrating problems. But if what you're saying doesn't resonate with who's reading it, your perfectly crafted copy won't give you the conversions you need. It all still boils down to how much you understand your persona, and how relevant your copy is to them.

The You Language

"People aren't interested in you, they're interested in themselves."

– Dale Carnegie

Whether you're writing copy for your own business or for a client, and whether you choose to follow the AIDA or the PAS formula, don't forget exactly who your copy is intended for – your target audience.

What would they want to hear or read?
Why should they listen to you?
What's in it for them?

Reverse the roles and evaluate yourself as a consumer. How do you choose which ads, social media posts, or articles you pay attention to?

Let's say you're visiting New Jersey for the first time and stumble upon a list of the best restaurants in town. Which of these two are you most likely to check out first?

Restaurant 1:
We're one of New Jersey's finest restaurants, offering the best pizzas in town. Our award-winning dishes are from our own family recipes, passed down from generation to generation. Visit us for authentic Italian cuisine. We look forward to welcoming you into our home!

Restaurant 2:
Are you searching for the best pizza in town? You're welcome to visit our home for a taste of authentic Italian cuisine. Our award-winning dishes are from our own family recipes, passed down from generation to generation. One bite and you'll discover why we're one of Jersey's finest restaurants!

Based on the psychology of consumers and best marketing practices, Restaurant 2 should be more effective. Why? It's because of simply shifting the focus from the business, to the customer.

Let's go back to the quote shared earlier – people are interested in themselves. Put yourself in your target audience's shoes and focus on what they want. Both examples are technically saying the same thing, but the second restaurant utilizes the YOU language.

By simply using more YOUs, and less Is or WEs, you have more chances of building an instant connection with your reader. Filling your copy with Is and WEs is like that friend who keeps talking about themselves at the party, and won't even bother to ask how you're doing. It's one-way, distant, and can get really annoying, fast.

Drill #6

Here's an example of the copy written for the "About Us" section of website.com, a company offering web development services:

> We believe everyone deserves to have a website or online store. Innovation and simplicity make us happy: our goal is to remove any technical or financial barriers that can prevent business owners from making their own website. We're excited to help you on your journey!

Try adding more YOUs and tweaking the overall copy to make it more conversational. Even if it's "About

Us," your job as a copywriter is to somehow still make it about your customers. Something like this would build a better connection:

> *You deserve to have a website or online store. If innovation and simplicity make you happy, then we're on the same page. Our goal is to remove any technical or financial barriers that can prevent you from making your own website. We're excited to help you on your journey!*

Rather than putting the spotlight on the company, and talking about conceptual customers (they), why not speak directly to your market? Even if you're talking to the general public, readers would appreciate and respond more if they feel like your copy is intended specifically for them. Make your readers feel special.

Here's another example:

> *Our clients put thought into the products they make, the items they sell, the blog articles they write, or the software they build. We believe that makes us a good fit for each other. Our clients care deeply about the products and/or services they offer. It is safe to say that quality is their top priority. Doing what we love lies on finding the right client partners. We are dedicated to finding the ideal people to work with. People who put importance on their craft, design, value our input, and are authentic individuals. It is unfortunate that we have to turn down many potential work, as we have to decline the wrong fit, allowing us to work with the right fit. That's how we're able to come in each day with smiles on our faces.*

Sounds like a great company that's very proud of their current customers – but as a prospective client, I'm not quite sure if I'm welcome to get in touch with them... Try rewriting this in the You Language and see what happens.

> *As our client, we value how much thought you put into the pizza you make, the tea you sell, the blog you write, or the software you build. That's what makes us a good fit together. You care deeply about the products you offer or the services you provide, and quality is your top priority. Doing what we love hinges on finding the right client partners, so we're dedicated to finding the ideal people to work with – clients like you who value your craft, value design, value our input, and also happen to be nice, genuine humans. This means we turn down a lot of potential work – we say no to the wrong fit, so we can say yes to the right fit – and we hope, that's you. So, we can both go to work each day with smiles on our faces.*

See how much warmer, inviting, and more engaging it is now? I'd much rather talk to these guys than the ones earlier!

Who knew three letters could make such a drastic difference to your copy? Remember, copywriting isn't meant to be a monologue. Don't just talk. Talk to your customers, and give them a chance to respond with a conversion.

Coffee Talks

Here's another technique to keep your copy in check – talk to your customers as if you're chatting with a friend in a coffee shop.

Imagine this: You're at your neighborhood café, totally chill, enjoying your cup of joe, and settling in to start working on your copy. You suddenly see a familiar face walk by – It's a buddy you haven't seen in a while. You immediately invite them over and start catching up. *"What are you up to? What are you working on?"*, they ask. You tell them about the upcoming launch and they're interested to know more about this new phone. *"Oh cool, tell me more about it!"* How would you answer them? What would your conversation be like? Hold that thought – We'll get back to this later.

Write Like You Speak

Conversational writing is quickly becoming the language in business as well. With the power and prevalence of social media, the wall between brands and customers have been broken. The more accessible, sociable and personable your brand voice is, the better.

Write about your product or service as if you're explaining it to a friend. Remember how excited you were about something you've been dying to buy, and you told your friends all about how cool it was, and why you needed it in your life? Hold on to that thought and replicate it in your copy.

Keep it casual, even if you're trying to sell a serious product.

Here's how:

- Even if your copy is intended for thousands of people, only write for one person. This goes back to the *You Language* – make each reader feel like you're just talking to them, and they have your full attention.
- Keep it simple. Use short sentences and avoid complex words. This will make your copy easier to absorb. When you're done writing, review your work and try replacing bigger words with simpler ones. Copywriting isn't a vocabulary contest – It's not about using the best words you know, but the words your customer understands.
- Like in any good conversation, keep it two-way and ask questions. This also helps you avoid the *Me, Myself and I* type of writing, and makes your copy more engaging.
- Your English teacher might hate you for this, but go ahead and make use of contractions. This keeps your copy fluid and natural. Use *let's, you're, aren't...* Otherwise, you'll sound like a robot.

When you're done writing, here's the one thing you must do to truly nail a convincing, non-salesy copy: Read it out loud. This is the best way to check your overall tone and flow. If it sounds like something you'd naturally say – awesome!

Drill #7

Let's go back to the coffee shop scene. How would you tell your friend about this new phone that your client will launch next month? Start writing. Imagine what their follow-up questions might be, and continue writing. See where your conversation takes you, and read it out loud.

Conversations Lead to Conversions

Who are you most likely to listen to? Someone you met at a party telling you about a new phone they heard about, or the sales guy at the phone shop telling you about their new product launch next month?

Writing your copy should be as effortless as slipping it in a conversation at a party. It's not hard sell, not aggressive, no salesy at all. Consumers have evolved and appreciate being treated as a peer or a friend, as opposed to just being one of the many anonymous receivers of your message.

Conversational copy makes your writing more genuine, personal, and engaging, so it helps you build rapport with your target audience. It' a lot easier to understand, too, especially for long formats (like an e-book!).

So, when in doubt, go back to your imaginary coffee shop. Talk to your imaginary friend and see how your copy fits in your conversation.

CHAPTER 4: THE BATTLEFIELD

It's time to put your new-learned skill to the test.

You're now armed with the fundamentals and trade secrets of copywriting. While everything you've learned so far are basic principles for any type of copy, some guidelines may be more applicable than others for
specific copy requirements.

In this chapter, you'll try your hand at copy-specific drills. Consider this as a refresher course when you're about to take on a certain type of material. Some of the tips in the following pages may seem repetitive at times – Again, they're mere reminders of how you can best apply what you've learned in *The Boot Camp* and *The Big Guns*. Once you've nailed down those two chapters, it's much easier to see how you can apply certain strategies and tactics to different types of copy.

For each exercise, remember your training:
- Map out your plan of action first. Create a persona, identify your product benefits, translate these to emotional benefits with power words, and craft a compelling call to action.
- Choose a formula to follow and write in conversational style using the You Language.
- Read your copy out loud, and revise as needed.

You can now unload all the knowledge you've stashed in your armory.

Ready. Aim. Fire!

Ads and Headlines that Stick

First impressions last. And with any copy, your first sentence should stick – attract, entice, seduce your reader to click, read, open or share.

Headlines – well – head line your ads, social media posts, articles and just about everything else you write. Your opening statement has one goal: To get your first sentence read. Your body copy shall do the rest.

Here are the Four Effective U's to help you get started. Make sure your headline ticks one of these boxes:

- **Urgent –** A sense of urgency in your ad or article's headline helps make sure that they get noticed and acted on *now*, instead of having it saved for later. Coz let's face it – Even with Facebook's save feature, or your browser's bookmark function, you often forget to get back to them later. Use your explosive power words and pepper your headline with *today, right now, quick, asap* or *this summer* – and highlight what your readers might miss out on if they don't act *this instant*.

- **Unique –** Write in a fresh and surprising way. If it suits your product's brand voice, be as creative as you want to be. Take Buzzfeed's headlines for example. Instead of simply saying *The Top Ten Shows This Season* they might say something along the lines of *Binge-worthy Shows You Should Def Watch This Weekend Coz You*

Don't Have a Life or *Top Ten Shows This Season for People Who Crave More Drama in their Life – That's You BTW.*

- **Ultra-specific** – This one takes its cue from *How to Lose a Guy in 10 Days* and your usual *Lose 10 lbs in 14 Days.* People love being offered something quick and easy. Again, your role is to be the bearer of good news and the answer to their biggest problems. While *How to be a Successful Entrepreneur* presents a good solution, *How to be A Successful Entrepreneur, Be Your Own Boss and Quit Your Job in 30 Days* definitely sounds better!

- **Useful** – Sometimes, all you need to do is offer help. No tricks, no buzzwords, just an honest to goodness solution. It boils down, once again, to how much you know your persona, so your simple yet useful headline can resonate strongly with them. *5 Time Management Tools to Help you be More Productive at Work,* or *Simple Exercises You Can Do Even While Sitting Down* could be all they really need right now.

Once you've determined which of these U's would suit your copy requirements best, here are a few other tips to make sure you never write a boring headline again!

- Ask a question. It grabs attention and makes your reader want to read some more to find the answer.
- Include numbers. They're eye-catching and can break a monotonous headline.

- Make a bold claim. Again, your copy's all about being *the* solution your customers have been dying for. Own it!
- But, don't go for clickbait. Don't overpromise in your headline then underdeliver in the rest of your content. You need to build a genuine connection.
- Write at least 20 headlines. It's great exercise to get your creative juices flowing. See what you come up with, which one you like best, or perhaps, you can even mix and match some lines to zone in on your winning headline!

Drill #8

Rewrite the following headlines in four ways: Make each one an urgent, a unique, an ultra-specific, and a useful version, and try incorporating the other tips above!

- Parents Tweet the Darndest Things
- The Top Ten Must Try Restaurants in Town
- The App You've Been Waiting for Your Whole Life is Finally Here

---

Emails that Make You Click

Standing out in an over-crowded inbox is a challenge. Just imagine how many newsletters your target customers have signed up for – and how many offers, reminders, and notifications they receive each day. How can you make them notice you?

Here are some best practices on how you can get your recipients to open, read, and click on your email:

- **Make the most of your subject.**
Similar to a headline, your email's subject should make a great first impression. Keep it simple, but descriptive and straight to the point. Avoid any sales jargon, buzz words, and spammy words such as *sale*, *help* and *percent*. Most of all, don't use a clickbait that has nothing to do with the content of your email. Spend time thinking, writing and revising your subject – Make it sound like an email from a friend.

- **Choose formulas over templates.**
Email templates force you to adhere to their format, while formulas are much more fluid and can be tailored for your specific audience. Remember AIDA and PAS? Emails are one of the best channels to use them as you have more room to talk about benefits and solutions. See which one fits your product or email campaign better.

- **Be personal.**
Simply addressing your recipient goes a long way. *Hi [name]* is most likely to get your customer scrolling and reading more, as opposed to opening with *Hi everyone*. Remember – write as if you're just talking to one person, and make each customer

feel special. If you write to everyone, you write to no one. Use the You Language and keep the rest of your email body casual, much like a natural conversation. All The Big Guns play a crucial role here! It also helps if the sender has a name, instead of just the company name.

- **Keep it concise.**
  You may feel tempted to keep rambling in an email, thinking you have more space and time, compared to an ad for example. Despite of its more flexible medium, however, it's still best to keep your email copy short and straight to the point. Any sales copy is meant to propose a solution, remember? So best to get to that part right away. If you have lots of copy points to cover, use bullet points – It will be much easier for your reader to absorb everything at a glance.

- **Repeat your call to action.**
  Don't be afraid to repeat your call to action. Many businesses make the mistake of only leaving a button at the bottom or end of an email. If you can integrate this at the start and main body of your email as well, all the better. It doesn't always have to be the same button, too – find other ways of phrasing the same CTA. You already had some practice earlier, you got this!

Drill #9

Write a sample EDM inviting your target customers to the launch of your client's new phone. Incorporate the tips shared above – Be sure to have a couple of subject options, and have a personal, concise, and conversational email body with an effective formula and compelling calls to action.

You may have heard or encountered other email marketing tips such as the character limit for your subject, or when the best time for an email blast is. But here's the most important thing to remember – Copywriting is a social science based on human behavior. There are no one-size-fits-all template to follow. The best thing you can do is try out different tactics, keep testing, and see which is most effective for your brand and target market.

When everything's said and done, copywriting really is about a lot of practice. Just keep writing, testing, and learning, and forming compelling sales copy will eventually come easily and intuitively to you.

Product Descriptions that Sell

Describing a product seems like a pretty simple task. All you have to do is see, touch, smell, hear or taste it. As a copywriter, you're also often provided with reference materials to help you flesh out your copy. Even a paperclip can be described in various ways – its size, color, flexibility, material used, and so on. The challenge, however, is in making your paperclip *the* paperclip that your customer should buy.

When it comes to product descriptions, it's often tempting to simply list down all the technical specs. How many e-commerce websites have you encountered that just show you all the product features? It's great to know that Blanket A has a higher thread count than Blanket B, or that Refrigerator A is an Inverter, and Refrigerator B isn't – but what does that mean exactly?

In Chapter 2, we discussed the difference between product features and benefits, and how the latter leads to a greater emotional hook. It's this hook that provides a better chance for conversion.

In this section, we'll revisit the Boot Camp once again and explore other effective methods for writing compelling product descriptions.

- **Focus on your buyer.**
  Always keep your persona in mind. Imagine selling your product to them face-to-face, or just having a conversation with them at a coffee shop. What's their language – their humor, expressions, tone and personality? What would their questions be? How would they react to your answer? Take that conversation to your website and apply it on your product descriptions.

- **Translate your product features to benefits.**
  As a copywriter, it's important to fully immerse yourself in the brand or business you're writing for. Chances are you've written other types of copy for them, you know their products or services by heart,

and their jargon and technical features have been your second language. Problem is, this may be totally alien to your customer. List down each feature of your product, and write a corresponding benefit that would resonate with your target buyer. How can each feature benefit them in their daily lives or current frustrations?

- **Don't just sell the product, sell the experience.**
Avoid relying on salesy phrases such as *superior quality* or *the best in the market*. As soon as your market sees this, it's easy for them to dismiss your copy as just another pitch they've seen from other products before. It's a generic claim. Be specific. Paint a clear picture of the possibilities of how much easier, happier, or more successful their lives can be because of your product feature. Instead of simply mentioning that this shampoo has green tea extract, this facial wash has acne-combatting ingredients, or this toothpaste has intense peppermint flavor that lasts...Sell the promise of confidence.

- **Support your claims.**
Highlighting the benefits doesn't mean disregarding the specs and features. It's best to have a combination of both, where the features support the benefits. If you claim to be the fastest, the strongest, or the most advanced – Prove it. Write your benefits in the most enticing way, then back it up with your list of features. Having testimonials on your product page

is also a great way to do this, especially if it includes an image of the reviewer, or a snippet from social media.

- **Tease your customer's imagination.** It's a lot easier to sell a product your customers can see, touch, and test. Unfortunately, you don't have this privilege when writing product descriptions for the web. Great news is, you can always appeal to their imagination. Flex those copywriting muscles. Go back to your power words, and combine these with sensory words. Make your copy as descriptive, detailed and vivid as possible. Start with *imagine* and fill the rest of your copy with words like *crunchy, crisp, smooth, velvety, rich*. These will definitely help your readers have a taste of your product, or experience your service, even if it's just through their screens.

Different products may present different challenges, but the basic principles of an effective sales copy will always take you back to The Boot Camp. Simply understand your persona and sell them a powerful emotional benefit.

Website Copy that Converts

A website is now every brand's most important digital asset. It's a hub of all the information they need their target audience to know. For location-based businesses, it's an extension of their physical shop. Whether it's a simple portfolio website of specialized services or an e-commerce site of various products, the goal isn't to fill it with as much information as possible. It's to convert.

The key to writing persuasive web copy is clarity. From how you structure your content, to your choice of words, your visitors need to understand exactly what you're trying to say, where you want them to click, and what you want them to do. Here's how:

- **Write for your target audience.**
  Yes, as always, you need to start writing by going back to your persona. This is the only way you can craft your copy to give them exactly what they're looking for, in a way that's specifically easy for them to absorb. Different audiences have different needs, questions, priorities, tone of preference and trigger words – and your website copy should adjust accordingly.

- **Be a trust-worthy problem-solver.**
  The more you know about your customer, the more you can anticipate their problems and concerns. Welcome them to your site with your solution. Focus on your features and benefits, and address any bottlenecks they may have. You can do this by integrating elements that build trust such as testimonials, reviews, case studies, press coverage, and product ratings. You can also throw in risk-free offers in your call to action such as *cancel anytime*, *free trial*, and *money back guarantee.* All these features will ease your web visitors and help them overcome any doubts or hesitations they may have.

- **Get to the point.**
  You only have three seconds to hook your web visitors when they land on your website. Instead of opening with a witty headline just for the sake of being witty, or some splashy animation, present your most important copy points right away. Help your visitors find what they need, as quickly as possible. An overly animated or cluttered website may chase away potential customers who simply need an immediate answer. Also stick with short and simple, yet clever and creative copy. No industry jargon and no complex words. When in doubt, it's always safe to imagine that you're reading your website copy to grade school kids.

- **Keep it conversational.**
  As discussed in Chapter 3, even if a website is technically about a business, you should shift the attention to your customers and find a way to still make it seem about them. Talk to them, always utilize the YOU Language and avoid Is, WEs and THEYs. Go back to the coffee shop scene, and imagine having a casual chat with them. Keep the conversation two-way – Ask questions, which immediately prompts an interaction.

- **Show personality.**
  Your website will serve as your best representation online. Even if your copy is focused on your customers, you can still show your brand's personality in your writing style. Determine your overall tone and brand voice, and keep it consistent

throughout your site. Aside from your products and services, it's your personality that will set you apart from your competition and allow you to make a good impression.

Web Content Formatting Guidelines

Aside from keeping your copy clear and customer-driven, here are a few other formatting guidelines to help shape your copy for higher conversions:

- Consider scanability and write for skimmers by breaking down your content into headings and sub headings.
- Try to keep your paragraphs to four sentences or less.
- Try to keep your sentences to twelve words or less.
- Include links to other pages of your website, especially your goal URLs or conversion pages.
- Always clearly tell your visitors what to do next – *click here, download now, sign-up today* – and apply tips on writing compelling calls to action.

Onsite SEO

It's no secret that writing for the web is ruled by keywords. It's definitely recommended that you integrate your target keywords in your copy – but do so in the most natural way. Only include them if they seamlessly fit in the conversation. Never insert keywords just for the sake of having them there.

Here's a rule of thumb when it comes to optimizing your copy – Write for your readers first, and Google second. Don't get hung up on SEO writing guidelines. Always focus on your reader. They're online searching for solutions. The more you appeal to your customers and give them the content they need, they more you'll appeal to Google's algorithm. Always ask yourself, *How else can I be more helpful to my reader?* If you address this correctly, your website's conversion and optimization will follow.

Landing Pages that Hit the Mark

In the previous section, we talked about general web copy guidelines to help convert your web visitors to customers. While any sales copy should focus on conversion, landing pages are specifically created just for this purpose.

By now, you've already mastered the basic principles of conversion-driven copy. So, in this section, we'll tackle specific copy points for you to focus on when A/B testing your landing pages.

- **Your headline** – Go back to the different headline styles you've learned. Try a different style, or try replacing your power words. Add some numbers, or more creative phrases. You could also try switching your bold statement with a question instead. Write 20 more options, assess, mix and match, and test. Remember, you need to start strong to allow the rest of your copy to do their job.

- **Your call to action** – Is your CTA clear, enticing enough, and evident? Similar to your headline, you may want to try different styles and power words as well. Perhaps you could make it sound more urgent, or throw in a risk-free offer? Or sometimes, this may not even be a copy issue. See if modifying your CTA button may do the trick. Perhaps its style, color, or position may need some adjustment? It could all boil down to the smallest detail, such as your choice of font!

- **The amount of information provided** – Compared to the rest of your website copy, your landing page should focus on content for a specific campaign. Perhaps it's too concise and you haven't provided enough information to convince them of your product's value? Or maybe there's too much information for them to process? Review the significance of every copy point you have, and assess if there's anything missing or irrelevant. Again, this could also boil down to design and layout. Is it too cluttered? Is there a better way to visually present all the information you have?

- **Possible objections** – Revisit your persona. Review the bottlenecks you identified or possible objections to using your product or service. Were you able to address them in your landing page? Are there other possible sources of hesitation that you can think of? Or perhaps you're not addressing their most pressing concern?

- **Trust elements** – Are there enough trust elements in your landing page? Should you make the testimonials or ratings more evident? Is there a new review from a credible source that you can feature? Are your trust elements believable and easy to verify? Or are there better testimonials that you can use? Perhaps the ones you have now aren't really addressing your persona's main challenges, or they just seem to be generic statements?

Landing pages can be tricky. The problem and solution may either lie in your copy, on the overall layout, design, or a combination of different elements. What's important to remember is to test, and test some more. You may think that your landing page is already performing well, but you wouldn't really know unless you try changing different variables, and see how that affects your conversion. There might not even be a problem, but just other ways to make it better!

Conclusion

Congratulations! You're now licensed to kill... in copywriting, of course.

In a nutshell, good copy puts the customer first, and presents an immediate solution as effortlessly as possible, to persuade them to take a specific action.

It starts with understanding your target audience – their needs, wants, and challenges – which often requires not just a practical, but an *emotional* answer.

Highlight a benefit instead of product specifications, focus on value instead of price, and trigger emotion instead of just reason. This is where the power of words comes into play.

Know the challenges you can solve, understand the bottlenecks you need to overcome, and revel in the dreams you can help fulfill – That's how you accomplish your mission.

Discover more at my website.

https://wswainbrand.com/

Killer Copywriting Reloaded

The Advanced Guide on How to Write Copy That Sells

Disclaimer

Reasonable care has been taken to ensure that the information presented in this book is accurate. However, the reader should understand that the information provided does not constitute legal, medical or professional advice of any kind.

No Liability: this product is supplied "as is" and without warranties. All warranties, express or implied, are hereby disclaimed. Use of this product constitutes acceptance of the "No Liability" policy. If you do not agree with this policy, you are not permitted to use or distribute this product.

We shall not be liable for any losses or damages whatsoever (including, without limitation, consequential loss or damage) directly or indirectly arising from the use of this product.

Table of Contents

Introduction

Chapter 1 A Refresher

Chapter 2 Tackling the Brief

Chapter 3 Getting In The Zone

Chapter 4 Branding with Words

Chapter 5 Digital Marketing

Chapter 6 Scribe Support

Conclusion

Introduction

The fact that you're reading this book means you have survived the basic copywriting boot camp. You already know the nuances of good copywriting and you may have developed some skills in writing a persuasive copy. But you and I know that it's a business jungle out there and basic skills can only get you so far. You don't only need more writing ammunition, but you also need new weapons to add to your copywriting arsenal.

Learning advanced skills will prepare you to become competitive in the ever-changing business and marketing landscape. If you arm yourself with advanced copywriting skills, you can move with the times and you can buck the digital trends. It doesn't matter who you write for or what platform you use, if you master copywriting, you'll always stay relevant.

But before you enter the war room, a refresher is in order. If you have not put your copywriting skills into practice for so long, chances are your copywriting is as dead as a doornail—nothing a quick refresher can't fix. Get to it and then I'll see you in the war zone!

.

Chapter 1 A Refresher

What is Copywriting?

Copywriting is the craft of creating persuasive messages that compel people to take action—purchase a product, download an eBook, donate to a cause, vote for a candidate, or follow on Twitter—you get the idea.

In the realm of marketing and advertising, copywriting is an extremely important skill to have because it is how businesses send their messages to audiences across different platforms. Do it right and you'll help reach even the loftiest business goals but do it wrong and you'll suffer the negative consequences.

With copywriting, words are used not just to inform, impress or tantalize, but to sell. Unlike typical writing, copywriting's main intention is to sell something, whether it be a product, a service, a cause, or an idea.

You know the ads you see on billboards and the commercials you watch on TV? That's copywriting at work. So, when you watch a commercial and you feel compelled to take action, remember that a copywriter wrote the script to get you to do exactly just that. Powerful stuff, right?

To better understand copywriting, you must look at it as a process with different stages. As with any process, copywriting has a beginning and an end. It starts by setting a goal. When a goal is established, the next step is identifying the target audience and studying their behavior. This is then followed by identifying which medium or platform to use. The actual writing can only take place after all these factors are identified and understood.

In copywriting, words are the currency worth their weight in gold. Powerful words are used to trigger an emotional response. When carefully chosen words are weaved together to get the desired reaction, you can expect your audience to have an emotional connection to the copy. The writing can stir up strong emotions and spark the desire to do something. With that said, the choice of words can make or break a copy.

The goal of copywriting is not just to sell, but to sell better. Copywriting not only creates awareness of a product, service, or brand, but it can turn awareness to actual sales. How you use words to structure your copy can influence audience behavior. So, in that sense, you can actually create the outcome you desire, which is to sell better.

When aligned with marketing goals, copywriting can help achieve your desired outcomes. You'll know how you're faring when you're either feeling the thrill of victory or the agony of defeat.

Evolution of Copywriting

Copywriting has been an integral part of advertising and marketing campaigns throughout history. Before the world wide web existed, businesses simply put out advertisements on radio, TV, and print media. The purpose was to inform people about a product or service and to compel them to make a purchase or make use of the service. The intent was two-fold: enticing the audience and convincing them that one brand is better than the other.

Copywriters of the past specialized in advertorial copywriting and they work as part of creative ad agencies. Independent or freelance copywriters were unheard of at that time. Copies were worded as straight-up advertising and consumers know and feel that they are being sold t0. There was never any doubt that the materials written were sales ads through and through.

When the internet happened, copywriting changed drastically. It's as if traditional advertising and online media got married and had a baby. Digital copywriting was born, and copywriters were all caught in a digital maelstrom that is still happening to this day. Goals have changed and copywriters have been given more roles (and more work!). The world communicates differently, and messages are now being sent to audiences instantly. As a result, the response is also immediate—good or bad.

The dynamics between businesses and consumers have changed significantly. Consumers now tend to engage more with digital ads and less on conventional ad copy. They also consume content in different ways so there's no guarantee that a copy would evoke the same reaction from all consumers.

Modern copywriting is more about building relationships. It's no longer an in-your-face sales pitch, but more of a value-driven spiel. If a copy could effectively show consumers that there is real value to what is being offered, whether it be a product or a service, then it is considered successful.
But even if copywriting strategies and methods have changed, the foundation of effective copywriting remains the same. It's still about identifying your

target audience and getting in their head so that they are compelled to take action.

Copywriting still relies heavily on emotions. Words are still written in such a way that they grab attention immediately and stir up all sorts of emotions. And of course, correct grammar and spelling still matter no matter the chosen medium.

Importance of Copywriting

Businesses today want to create a positive brand image and experience. This can be achieved by using a holistic approach that includes copywriting. It is only through effective copywriting that businesses can send the message they want to communicate to their respective audiences.

Copywriting is important in any business because it is a tool to drive consumer response that could eventually lead to the desired end goal—purchase! When effectively written, copywriting can convince consumers that there is a unique benefit in buying the product or in utilizing a service.

The words can offer a strong proof that the product or service fulfills a need. It tells consumers that they stand to benefit from using the product or from availing the service. More importantly, it can guide the consumers to make a snappy decision to buy. Without copywriting, there's nothing to guide consumers on what to do next.

Copywriting is not just limited to promoting products and services, it can also be used to sell ideas, change opinions, win arguments, or influence decisions. Just imagine what you can do if you have the copywriting skills and instincts:

- Convert consumer engagement to sales
- Convince headhunters that you are the right person for the job
- Sell an idea that opposes conventional belief. (If flat earthers can do this, so can you.)
- Convince angel investors to fund a business venture
- Persuade strangers to fund your latest project through crowdfunding
- Convince a swing voter to vote for your chosen political candidate
- Prove that your idea is better than what the team decided to pursue

Copywriting essentially makes you a master manipulator using words as your weapon of choice to sweet-talk people into yielding to your own ideas and opinions. And if you master the craft of copywriting, getting your desired results is just cake walk.

Your Role as a Copywriter

As a modern copywriter, you have additional roles to play, more hats to wear, and new things to do, but you still retain the distinctive skills and traits of the copywriter from days of old. The basic foundation of what makes a copywriter great is still the same— skillful use of words to persuade and the ability to tell a compelling story.

Digital copywriting is no longer limited to just creating content that introduces and sells products. Your role as a copywriter has expanded beyond the traditional functions because people are now choosing the kind of content they want to consume. If they want to read about a product, they would read blogs. If they want to see products, they would go to Instagram. If they would rather watch videos, they would turn to YouTube. There is a variety of platforms to consider and every copywriter who is worth her salt would recognize the opportunity in using each of these mediums.

Each social media platform has its own nuances, so each copy must be tailored-fit to take advantage of the digital quirks. What works in one medium, may not necessarily work with another. In this sense, your role as a copywriter involves figuring out how the same content can be communicated in several ways without losing the key message.

Templates had worked before in radio, TV, and print media, but they don't work the same way they do on social media. That's why you, as a copywriter, have to learn the intricacies of blogging, Search Engine

Optimization (SEO), internet marketing, social media advertising, content writing, and ecommerce, among other things.

You still with me?

I'm not even going to lie, but yes, the different roles you have to play can be overwhelming and daunting. But before you start crawling up into a fetal position, just know that all these things will make sense as you get to the later chapters. You must trust the process. The growth in ecommerce is nothing short of amazing. Anyone with an idea and some cash can set-up an online business almost instantly. The barriers to entry are almost non-existent. Everything is now automated that businesses can operate with only a few employees and staff. Business is now a level playing field.

The competition is not solely about the products anymore—there is a content war going on. Let me explain. Since businesses now have an online presence, the battle is on how to get potential customers to take notice.

With the change in business landscape, advertising and marketing must also change. And since copywriting is the hallmark of a great marketing campaign, it follows that copywriting must also be tweaked drastically.

Since we are living in a digital world, copy ads are available 24/7. People are inundated with content everywhere they look. It would be impossible for people to read all the content available online, so they become discerning and selective of the content they consume online.

They are no longer the push-over consumers who are being sold products to. They are now informed consumers and they rely on internet searches for their next purchase.

The modern consumers are research-driven. Their online shopping destination are based on the terms they type on the Google search bar (or some obscure search engines they use).

As a copywriter, you must adapt to the new digital marketing landscape. You must then be aware that the work scope has expanded to cover pretty much anything that involves the written word. You'll find yourself writing copy for any or all of the following and for various platforms.

- Articles for content marketing
- Banner ads
- Blog posts
- Brochures
- E-books
- Email marketing or newsletter
- Flyers
- Google ads
- Industry reports
- Infographics
- Posters
- Presentations
- Press releases
- Proposals
- Sales letters
- Social media ads
- Social media profiles
- Social media updates
- Splash pages or sales pages
- Tagline
- Video scripts
- Website

The list is by no means exhaustive. If the latest digital marketing trends are any indication, people will certainly find new ways to send messages across. This is great news for copywriters because their services will be more in-demand because of the special set of skills they possess.

Everywhere you look, you see the manifestation of the power of words. When combined with design and technology, words can entice and compel people to ask about the brand or the product, at the very least. The role of the copywriter is to find the right words that would not only pique the consumers' curiosity, but also spark genuine interest that can be converted to sales or other measure of success.

If you are a copywriter who trained and worked the traditional way, you might find yourself struggling to adapt to the new methods and techniques. Don't be discouraged. It's all part of the learning process. Although copywriting has shifted massively to the digital medium, it doesn't mean that its foundation has changed. If your fundamentals are sound, the transition would not be as difficult as might appear to you. One way to convince you that you are on the right path is to tell you that straight up that the digital medium is the ideal platform for the craft of copywriting.

Not convinced? Well, think of it this way, modern copywriting techniques are not relying solely on written words. Look around you. Every content is a combination of words and visuals. Images become stories when there are words that accompany them. Without words, photos and images tell only parts of the story. The whole story can only be presented through words. Even videos need copywriters. What you watch on YouTube may appear to be spontaneous and spur-of-the-moment videos, but the truth is that most of them follow a script or an outline at the very least. Product reviews, video reactions, how-to videos, and vlogs all follow a structure. Chances are, they have all been written or created with the help of a copywriter.

What this means really is that copywriting is as important as it has ever been. Copywriting is not an antiquated craft that is in danger of becoming obsolete. Arguably, copywriting is more important now because products and brands need to have a "voice" to engage consumers and turn them into paying customers. Based on how consumers are reacting and engaging with brands, the trend is towards copy that are more conversational and value-centric. In-your-face ads and blatant promotions no longer worked as effectively as they used to.

Businesses are creating narratives to generate interest in their products and brands and who are better at weaving narratives than copywriters? With that said, the future belongs to copywriters who specialize in storytelling and in creating narratives that appeal to the emotions of the customers to hook them and never let them go.

Chapter 2 Tackling the Brief

Elements of a Brief

In copywriting, the creative brief is the write-up that sets the goal of the project and the necessary requirements to achieve that goal. It contains the background information about the project, the requirements, the expectations, the key performance indicators, and pretty much all the information that set the course of the project?

Is a brief really necessary? The only answer that matters is a resounding yes. I know that you are raring to get straight into the actual copywriting process but don't fall into that trap!

The business landscape has changed dramatically in the last few years and part of that change is the ability to reach out to clients no matter where they are in the world. Copywriting projects can now be done remotely. Very rarely do clients personally meet up with copywriters and micromanage their work. To create the copywriting gold, you need a detailed brief that will be your blueprint to produce exceptional content that produces results.

This cannot be rushed.

You might think that a short copywriting brief would be enough to cover what the project requires. While you have the option to write a short outline covering the general scope of work, it may cost you more time later on.
Let me explain.

If you only include the general structure of the project, you're potentially creating room for more questions to arise as you start to do the work. There will be more gaps to fill and if you do not have the right information, you and the client would go back and forth just trying to fill the gaps. It's time that should have been used more productively to create the killer copy.

Guesswork would not work either because it's a sure ticket to countless revisions. So, if you spend a reasonable amount of time to produce a detailed brief that has all the elements needed to keep the project moving in the right direction, then you can be assured that you'll meet or exceed expectations.

So, what exactly do you need to include in the copywriting brief?

- Project Description. This defines the project's goals and objectives and explains the methods and resources that would be used to execute the project.
- Scope and Inclusions. This defines the scope
- Goal. This describes what the project wants to achieve. In copywriting, it could be content that could create awareness or convert engagement to sales.
- Objectives. These are the specific steps that the copywriter must take to achieve the main goal or the desired outcome.
- Target Audience. This is the group or people or population that you are trying to engage. The client will have to determine this but it's up to you to do research about the audience and figure out how to relate to them using words.

- Call to Action. This is the specific actions you want your target audience to take after they've been engaged. The call to action doesn't always have to be a purchase; it could be as simple as joining the company's mailing list, sharing a post, liking a page or a post, or visiting a website.
- Tone and Style. The tone of the copy would have to match the brand or the product. You have to determine if it has to be written in an informal conversational, promotional, educational, friendly, or business-like manner. This will be determined taking into account the client's inputs.
- Deliverables. These are the materials that you are expected to produce. It could be one material or a set of materials that would cater to the nuances of the different social media platforms. It could be an email, a banner ad, a brochure, an infographic, or any material that the client requires. This also includes sizing information and versions.
- Deadlines. This is the exact time the copy needs to be submitted to the client or the time period the materials need to be sent out to the masses. Marketing campaigns usually have different phases that require specific materials. Campaigns that have limited-time offers require materials to be ready in advance. You must take into consideration that time it takes to finish the materials and the time it needs to be submitted.
- Constraints and Limitations. Sometimes, due to budget constraints, the copy would be limited in terms of word count or design. So, you have to know if you would be working with some limitations so that you can adjust your work to fit the specific requirements.

- Keywords. These are terms, words, or phrases that must be inserted in the copy as part of Search Engine Optimization (SEO) efforts. These keywords are vital to make sure that consumers will find the website, product, or brand when they do a Google search.
- Mandatory elements. These are specific requirements that the client wants added in the copy, no matter what. These are non-negotiable requirements that may or not fit into the overall conceptual. So, you have to make sure that they don't stick out like a sore thumb.

It would be wise to discuss the contents of the copywriting brief with your client before starting the project. This way, expectations would be managed and there will be no surprises come submission time. This also gives an opportunity for both parties to add, change, or remove any elements that don't fit the overall marketing strategy. There's a chance to work out the kinks while still in paper so that the copywriting can proceed with little interference.

In some way, a copywriting brief also provides some form of protection from clients who change their minds a lot and insist that you have agreed on something else entirely. Conversely, the brief also serves as a checklist for clients to ensure that they are getting your end of the bargain.

Having a copywriting brief is an essential part of the process that must not be ignored. It's a win-win situation for both you and your client when there is a document that sets out the copywriting objectives and the methods needed to execute to achieve them.

Target Audience vs. A Persona

In copywriting, part of the preparation is identifying your target audience. The target audience are the people that you are trying to reach. They are prospects you want to engage and the consumers who you want to offer your products or services to. Since they are the focus of your copy, you must tailor-fit your copywriting to target them.

But before you can do that, you have to ask yourself these four important questions:

- Who are you talking to when you write your copy?
- What information do you want them to know about your brand, product, or service?
- What do you want them to feel while reading your copy?
- What do you want them to do after they read your copy?

If you can answer these questions, you can effectively create a framework in which to create a persona.

What is a Persona?

In the realm of marketing, a persona is composite sketch of a segment of your target audience. It serves as a yardstick to which every target is measured against. It's the ideal person who would most likely want your product or service. It's putting a face, a name, and a background to the audience that you are writing for so that you are able to meet their needs.

A persona goes beyond demographics. It's more than just knowing the gender, the age bracket, the income level, or the educational attainment. It's stepping into their world and feeling what they feel and understanding why they behave the way they do.

By creating personas, you will be able to identify the appropriate language, tone, and style of your copy so that it would make sense to your target audience. If you get the pulse of your audience, you will be able to deliver content that will be relevant, useful, and valuable to them.

Creating A Persona

Before you start writing your copy, you must first create a persona (or
personas) that would be representative of your target audience. This exercise might be foreign to you, but the more you get into it, the more you'll find that it's a fun yet effective way to get to know your audience and potential customers. Now, get into character!

Step 1: Collect information

Creating a persona is no walk in the park, but if you know where to get your data and information, the process becomes a lot easier. The quality of the data you collect would depend on your sources. You already have a general idea of your target audience, but you need specifics. Here are ways you can collect information:

- **Interview people:**
  By interacting with people that belong in your identified target audience, you are getting information from the horses' mouth—and you can't get more accurate than that. The feedback

you get from them is an excellent source of information that can be used to form create a realistic and accurate persona.

- **Go Virtual:**
  The web is a treasure-trove of key information that will help you create a persona. Aside from the web analytics and the statistics, you can get a feel of how your target audience behave and interact online. You can read their feedback and product reviews and can easily determine the lifestyle that they lead.

- **Social Media Stalking:**
  What better way to get to know your target audience than following them on social media? The information you get from social media profiles and postings are useful in creating a persona. Because people reveal so much of themselves on different social media platforms, it's easy to analyze and study them from a marketing (and copywriting) perspective.

- **Make Assumptions:**
  I know you're thinking that assuming things is a recipe for copywriting disaster. While this is true for the most part, keep in mind that the assumptions being referred to here are informed assumptions. Do this when you have already been working with a product or brand for a reasonable amount of time—long enough to make informed and accurate assumptions.

- **Conduct Surveys:**
  A survey is a reliable source of data because it is designed to get answers to your research questions. With social media, it's easy to reach out to people that represent your target market. Online surveys make it easier to convince people to participate because the process doesn't eat up a lot of time. Don't forget to give them

incentives and rewards so that the survey would be worth their while.

You can use one method or a combination of these data gathering strategies to get the information you need to create your personas.

Step 2: Create Customer Subgroups

There's no standard number of personas to create, but you should end up with a number that would represent your customer subgroups. The target audience can be fairly diverse so if you can find a way to find the sweet middle spot, then you'll be certain to get an accurate representation of your audience.

One of the ways to do this is to divide and conquer. This means grouping your audiences into primary and secondary personas. The primary personas are customers that are important because they make an impact in terms of revenues and profits they bring. The secondary personas are those that don't have the same impact but they still contribute to the company's bottom line. Other groups that are too small or too specific can be eliminated.

Step 3: Set the Demographics

Once you're done with gathering data and segmenting your target audience, you can now set up the demographic information. These are details that include name, age, residence, marital status, and job. It also includes a photo to give each persona a face.

Step 4: Describe Persona Background

By describing the persona in terms of background, it adds a layer of insights into the target audience. This can include details about their job and their family life.

Step 5: Specify Persona Goals

Defining persona goals is necessary because it is a way to make you see how your copywriting goals align with the audience you are writing for. Having their goals out in the open can make you tailor fit your copy to meet their needs better.

Step 6: Define Persona Motivations and Pain Points

Motivation is what drives the customer to achieve their goals, while their pain points are the things that frustrate them the most. Defining their motivations and pain points can help you design your copy to inspire them to action and to provide solution to their problems.

Step 7: Add Other Elements

Sometimes the process of creating a persona stops at Step 6 because at that point, the personas can already give an accurate picture of the target audience. However, adding more elements into the personas make them even more complete. If you have more insights into your audience, there's no reason to add them to the personas. You can add skills, prior work experience, expectations, hobbies, social media presence, blogs they read, level of their computer literacy, quotable quotes from interviews, and other elements that can make your personas more real.

Win with Personas

By creating personas, you are immersing yourself into your target audience's world. You'll gain insights about your current and potential customers that would be pivotal in creating your copy. When you succeed in creating personas, you will benefit in the following ways:

- You will get maximum customer exposure because you'll develop empathy towards your customers.
- You will be able to identify your customers' true interests.
- You will get the pulse of your target audience with incredible accuracy that it would be easier to communicate with them.
- You and your audience will find a common language, which makes interaction and communication a breeze.
- You will be able to determine the kinds of improvements that customers want in the products they use. Your client will then be able to make better decision to improve their product.
- You can create a persuasive elevator pitch to your target audience because you know them inside and out.
- You can provide the solution that customers are looking and waiting for.

Drill #1

Create a persona for a new tablet that your client will launch next month. Here's guide you can use to help you get started:

Demographics	Age, gender, education, income, status?
Career Background	Industry, job, responsibility, career path?
Career Goals	More time, more income, more awards?
Skills	Technical skills, language skills, computer skills?
Personal Interests	What are their hobbies, where do they go often?
Attitude and Values	Are they health-conscious, eco-friendly, thrifty?
Motivations	What keeps them moving forward to achieve their goals?
Pain Points	What are their main frustrations?
Potential Bottlenecks	What could be their possible objections about using your product / service?

For the purpose of this exercise and the following drills throughout this e-book, here's our sample persona:

Trisha is a digital artist in her early 20s. She's a digital designer for an advertising company and works directly with copywriters and creative directors. She loves her job and enjoys working in a fast-paced industry. Even though she's satisfied in her work, she finds herself wanting to do more outside work that showcase her skills as a digital artist.

She needs to find an outlet for her creativity and she wants to focus more on digital art and animation. Luckily, being in the advertising industry has helped her build the right connections to land commission work. She wants to create a YouTube channel where she can showcase her digital masterpieces and provide digital art tutorials as a way to give back to the community.

Trisha needs a drawing tablet that can handle heavy digital processes the same way PCs do. Her options are limited and price prohibitive. She wants an assurance that the specs justify the price point. Her worst nightmare would be settling for a sub-par device.

Features vs. Benefits

With the target audience in mind, you have to ask yourself what you want them to know about the product or service you want to pitch to them. The knee-jerk reply is to list all the features that set the product or service apart from the competitors. You use superlatives (the most, the best, the fastest, etc.) to describe the features in the hope that they would drum up enough interest to actually convince them to purchase the product or make use of the service.

Features tell. Benefits sell.

Enumerating the features gives the consumer a clear idea of what the product in terms of its physical properties–the specs, color, size, materials, and other attributes that can be seen, touched, or tested.

There's really nothing wrong with this. In fact, every company does this. It's what makes customers identify and distinguish the product from a sea of other products available in the market. They might hook the customers if what they're looking for matches the physical specifications of the product. But what if they are looking for something else? What if they are having a difficult time deciding on what to buy? The features are not enough to convince them to make a purchase decision right there and then.

Enumerating the features in a robotic fashion just won't cut it. Sometimes, the features get too technical that they just go right over your customers' heads. They are just too much to handle. They will get bored and lose interest. And once they do, that's one less opportunity to get a sale.

Instead of telling the customers about the amazing features of the product, you tell them straight up how they will benefit from using the product. Remember the pain points in the persona that you have created? Use that to provide a solution to the problem and ease the pain. Since you already know what frustrates them, then find a way to remove those frustrations. The less frustrations they have, the closer they get to achieving their goals.

Customers want to know how using the product will help them in their day-to-day activities. If the product can make them work faster, they'll have extra time to do other things. If the product can remove extra steps in the work process, then they could finish the job with time to spare. If they can automate a tedious process, then they can do more and be more productive in a day. These are examples of benefits that would appeal to the customers.

Keep the amazing features in the copy but highlight the benefits of using the product. It's a deadly combination that will not only spark interest in the product, but also convert that interest into sales.

If you think that it sounds easy, that's because it is. You only need to be armed with knowledge of your customers' pain points and find the features that will help take away the pain. Features and benefits go hand in hand. But between the two, benefits can take most of the credit for influencing a purchase decision.

Here's a cool trick to help you turn basic features into key benefits – Simply ask, "So what?"

Drill #2

So instead of saying...

*This amazing new tablet weighs only 468g, with 12.9"
Liquid Retina display (2732 x 2048), 264 ppi display.
It's available in Black, Silver, Space Gray, White, and
Pink. It's powered by A12X Bionic chip, has 64-bit
architecture, with neural engine, and M12
coprocessor.*

*It has a 10,875MAh battery capacity and comes with
1TB internal storage and 6GB RAM. Best of all, it has
4K video recording at 30 fps or 60 fps with cinematic
video stabilization*

Break down the important features and ask yourself –
So what?

- *This amazing new tablet weighs only 468g.*
So what?
*It's the perfect size for a tablet that you can take with
you wherever you go.*

- *It's powered by A12X Bionic chip with 64-bit
  architecture, neural engine, and embedded M12
  coprocessor.*
So what?
*You get a powerful chip that allows you to multitask
when you work on a creative project.*

- *12.9" Liquid Retina display (2732 x 2048), 264
  ppi display.*
So what?

You get true-to-life color with gorgeous display. Every detail is captured.

- *It's available in Black, Silver, Gray, White, Gold, Bronze and Pink.*

So what?
With many options, you'll find one that matches your style.

- *It has a 10,875MAh battery capacity*

So what?
Your phone can finally keep up with the demands of your work.

- *Comes with 1TB internal storage and 6GB RAM*

So what?
You have more than enough storage space to save your digital artworks and videos.

- *Best of all, it has 4K video recording at 30 fps or 60 fps with cinematic video stabilization.*

So what?
You can showcase your digital artworks in high-quality cinematic format.

By asking "So what?", you are able to provide solutions to Trisha's pain points. These solutions will definitely get her attention and would be interested to know more about the product and most likely take the product home.

Context and Content

Life was much simpler when writers only had to worry about producing amazing content on various platforms. Many marketers subscribed to the idea that by simply churning out mind-blowing content, the product would get enough exposure and eventually, sales. While this was true back when blogs and social media were still in their infancy stage, it's only somewhat true today.

No one's contesting that content is important for marketing. Content is still king, but it has to be the right content communicated to the right people at the right time.

Enter Context Marketing.

Context marketing takes into account the target audience when delivering content. Whereas content just provides information in the hopes that someone from the target audience would take notice, context marketing zeroes in on the right audience to provide supremely relevant and personalized content.

You already know that the target audience should be at the forefront of your mind whenever you write your copy. What is less obvious is that you need to take into account how context could affect or influence the way your audience interact with your copy.

Even if you know your audience's demographics, motivations, and pain points, it is not wise to assume that you got your audience pinned down. If you write your content based on the personas you have created, it's still a hit or miss approach. But if you put context into your content, your copy affects them in a more profound way. With that said, you need to figure out where your words fit into your target audience's experiences.

How does context marketing manifest itself? How would it look like to you as a copywriter, if you have not utilized this approach in the past? Understanding the stages of inbound marketing and sales funnel can help you write a copy that has context which would grab your audience.

- **Top of the Funnel (ToFu)**
  At ToFu, it is safe to assume that your audience is not yet ready to buy whatever you're selling. There is a need to use some clever and snappy copy that will make readers pay attention. The copy utilizes a soft sell approach—light on details, but heavy on attention-grabbing content.

At this stage, you use your blogs, articles, and posts to provide information and make your audience understand your product. The audience here is largely potential leads that you want to convert into qualified leads, which have a higher chance of becoming actual paying customers.

This is the part where you know their pain points and you have the solution. The selling part is too subtle that you won't drive your audience away. You are still building a rapport so save the aggressive tactics for later use.

- **Middle of the Funnel (MoFu)**
  At this stage, you gently turn the volume up on the sales pitch by giving them information that will position the product as the solution to the challenges faced by the audience.

At this stage, you should continue to provide meaningful content but this time, you are positioning the product as the solution to the challenges of your leads. Advanced eBooks, exclusive content, and videos are the types of content that can help build your credibility.

- **Bottom of the Funnel (BoFu)**
  At the bottom of the funnel, you have engaged a healthy number of audience which are now valuable leads. They are already engaged and are comfortable interacting with the copy. Because you don't want to let go of them, you have to establish some urgency around making the purchase, so you offer them something that they could not refuse but they have to understand that it is a time sensitive offer. This is your direct call to action.

At this point, you step up to engage your leads one-on-one. There's less content, but more engagement. They are comfortable with you as you are comfortable with them. The most interested leads will respond well with your calls to action. You hook them with offers of trial, discount codes, or free assessments. Just don't lose the personal touch.

Context copywriting is using what you know about your target audience to speak to them in the language that they know well. When you use this strategy, you are guaranteed to achieve two important things:

1. **Personalized and relevant content**:
   When your copy is targeted at the needs of your audience, it becomes relevant to them. Your content would be meaningful and profound. When your content is personalized, it will get the attention of your audience, and creates an

opportunity to engage and lock them in long enough to respond to your call to action.

2. **Marketing performs much better**:
   When you employ context copywriting, you are delivering an effective content that is aligned to the marketing goals. And when the target audience respond well to the copy, the marketing campaign stands to reason that it will perform well.

Context copywriting is when your content meets or exceeds your target audience's expectations in a way that solves their problems or teaches them something new and valuable. It's content that caters to what your audience is looking for. It hooks them not because of clever writing, but because you offered them something that can change their lives for the better. That's the power of context marketing.

Scope of Work

The scope of work is a part of an agreement where the list of tasks to be performed are described. It is a contract between you and your client. The creative brief covers the scope of work, but it is more of your blueprint on how to accomplish the tasks. The scope of work, on the other hand, is what the client expects you to do and deliver and failing to do so could have repercussions.

It is similar in many ways to your creative brief, but it holds much more weight because it is a contract, whereas your brief is your blueprint. The scope of work provides details of the work including milestones, deliverables, timeline, and end products expected from you as a copywriter. It would all depend on what you and your client have agreed on.

Here are some of the things you need to keep in mind when creating or agreeing to a scope of work:

- The scope of work includes the work requirements that are clear and specific to avoid misunderstandings.
- It must include a glossary section where acronyms and terms are spelled out and defined. Think from the perspective of someone who is not from the same industry or discipline.
- Goals must be specific that they would leave no room for confusion and misinterpretation.
- The tasks must be aligned with the goals.
- The tasks must be measurable so that it can be evaluated based on key success factors.
- It must not be subject to different interpretations to avoid disputes after the work has been delivered.
- The deliverables must be detailed and itemized. It must also be specified if they are to be submitted in tranches or in one go.
- The deliverables are tangible outcomes so they must be quantifiable and measurable so that they can be evaluated upon the completion of the work.
- If the work is part of a time-sensitive marketing campaign, the timeline must be adjusted accordingly.

A clear and detailed scope of work will not only give a thorough picture of what the client expects of you, it will also serve as a document to help resolve issues and disputes should they arise along the way. It also removes ambiguities and uncertainties. Most of all, it protects your from unreasonable demands and it protects clients if the work fails to fulfill the requirements.

Chapter 3 Getting In The Zone

Not all copywriters are the same. Each has his or her own unique ways of getting into the writing zone. While some have pre-writing rituals, others search for inspirations that would jumpstart their writing engines. There's really no right or wrong way to do this; whatever works for them is a good thing. But there are techniques to help you get the creative juices flowing and craft the right content for your target audience.

The Power of Brainstorming

Sometimes, it's hard to be creative when you work with requirements and deadlines. They tend to limit your creativity because you have to conform to a structure and you have to complete the tasks at a specific time. More often than not, you're writing for a series of content for a marketing campaign in different social media platforms. You switch writing personas and change your tone just to churn out exciting and compelling content. But what happens when the creative juices stop flowing?

The simple answer is brainstorming.

You've heard about brainstorming for as long as you could remember, but do you practice it consistently before writing your copy? Maybe not as much as you should. Brainstorming harnesses the power of thinking out of the box. When you are stuck and your internal idea factory has shut down, brainstorming can help resuscitate your dying source of uniquely creative ideas. You can brainstorm on your own as part of your creative planning. But you can also brainstorm with a group if you feel that you really need some form of creative intervention.

Use brainstorming in any of the following scenarios:
1. You need new ideas that no one else has thought of before.
2. You ran out of ideas because you've used up all your idea cards in one go.
3. You have a problem to solve.
4. You want to extract ideas from other people. (This is especially useful if you work in a team and you want contribution from other members).

In copywriting, reasons 1, 2, and are most likely what got your attention. But how do you brainstorm? Do you sit and think about ideas all day long until something sticks? Do you talk to yourself hoping "yourself" talks back and comes up with something clever? Do you spy on competitors and see what they're up to?

While they may be considered loose forms of brainstorming, they don't usually get the desired outcome—to generate brilliant ideas. If you are going to do something anyway, might as well do it the right way. These brainstorming techniques are proven to keep your brain working on overdrive to spawn new ideas.

1. Play a game of associative brainstorming.

If you want to witness the power of associative brainstorming, play a word association game. Notice how you are able to think of other words that connect with one main word? That's your brain tapping into the subconscious so it spits out words that you know but never allow yourself to think under normal situations. The exercise allows you to go beyond typical thinking and opens the reserve fountain of unique ideas.

- **Word Storm.**
  This is a fun exercise where you conjure up a word storm by writing down the words that instantly come to your mind when you see another word.

To tailor-fit this brain exercise to your needs, you have to start with a word or a phrase that is directly related to your copywriting task. For example, you are working on a copy on a flash drive product. You can start with the word "flash" and think of words that you associate with it. You'll find that once you start, the words will come pouring.
The beauty of this exercise is that you just let your creativity flow because you're not overthinking. You'd be surprised at the words you'd think of when you're really not thinking too hard.

- **Mind Mapping**
  This is a way to organize data and information visually. You are able to better understand data and concepts because they are presented in colorful and memorable diagrams that are easy to follow.

A mind map represents your thought process, with the main idea as your primary thought. Other ideas relating to it are the secondary ideas that branch out. It is an effective way to get information in and out of your brain.

The great thing about mind mapping is that you are able to convert a huge amount of information into simple diagrams that will not overwhelm you. Complex concepts that are difficult to understand can be broken down into bite-size chunks that are more brain-friendly.

The final map might look like a city grid where all traffic leads back to the city center, which is your main idea. It looks like a total chaos, but it is an organized chaos that is within your control.

- **Word Banks**
  As a writer, you most likely know more words than the average person. Even if you possess the gift of words, there will be times when it's difficult to bring them out from the dark recesses of your mind. And when that happens, you tend to repeat the same words to prove a point.

Word banks help you find the right words that will perfectly suit your project. It's not enough to just find the synonyms of words, you have to find powerful words that can evoke an emotional response from people who read your copy.

You can create a collection of words that relate to your specific topic or theme. It will not only retrieve words that you already know but had only forgotten, but it can also expand your vocabulary by learning about new words you didn't know existed before you do the exercise.

- **Visual association**
  This is similar to word association but you use images to jumpstart your brain. Think of the Rorschach test, wherein a subject is asked to describe what ink blot images suggest or resemble. Visual association is pretty much the same, only you have to write down what you think when you look at an image.

Visual association can be done as part of the pre-planning stage of your project. You may look at an image of the product you are going to write about so you can be inspired by it or at least get some ideas out. You have complete control of this exercise because you choose the image or set of images you want to work with. As a rule of thumb, it's best to use images that relate directly to the product you are writing about.

This approach can also be used to evaluate the final copy or the marketing campaign as a whole. This way, the end product doesn't raise negative associations or controversies. It's a way to ensure that the public would not find something to criticize.

2. Use Measurable Brainstorming to Solve a Problem

There will be times when you will be faced with challenges and you need to make a decision. With problem solving brainstorming, you can think of different solutions, but you wouldn't know which one will solve the problem until you try all of them. Since there's no time for trial and error, what's left to do is to find the best solution among a list of solutions.

Measurable brainstorming allows you to come to an informed decision by utilizing the Pros and Cons method. This is a powerful tool when you want to weigh the positives and the negatives of a solution. The option that has the most pros would be the choice.

Although this approach is widely used and has its flashes of brilliance, it can easily be manipulated. It's not that you would cheat when you make your list, but there will always be an element of bias. To prevent this, you have to prioritize by importance. By putting more weight on things that help you achieve your goals, you are closer to getting to an informed decision, which, most of the time, leads to the best solution.

3. Shift Your Perspective

Associative brainstorming can help you clear the cobwebs from your mind so you can think with clarity and extract data from your brain. On the other hand, measurable and weighted brainstorming helps you prioritize and decide with confidence. However, sometimes, these approaches may not be enough and the information you have just don't spark creativity or generate groundbreaking ideas.

In situations like this, you have to do something different. You can't expect to achieve a different result if you keep doing the same thing over and over. To get you back on your creative track, you must shift your perspective to gain new insights and explore new possibilities.

- Ask questions. When you feel stuck, it doesn't hurt to ask questions. Sometimes, you may experience information overload which prevents you from generating ideas. Or on the other extreme, you are bombarded by creative ideas that you don't know how to execute them properly. They create creative noise that it drowns out the answers you are looking for.

When you ask questions, you get answers that help narrow down your options. It allows you to eliminate the non-integral parts of your process. It drowns out the noise and it leaves you with the answers that you need to get into the writing zone.

- "What If..." Asking this question opens up a long list of possibilities. It's like creating different alternative universes with different storylines and characters. Imagine the iterations of just one idea! With all the possibilities, you'll certainly find something that can work!

This is an effective way to shift your view significantly because you are thinking outside of the box and out of your comfort zone. You are given scenarios that are completely different from what you would expect so you are forced (in a good way) to change your perspective to understand the scenarios better. And from all the different alternatives, you can get ideas that will fit in your own created universe.

- Challenge Yourself by Thinking Prepositionally. Prepositions tell where an object is located. If you use a box as the location, you can use different prepositions to determine where an object is in relation to a box. The object could be in the box, under the box, or on top of the box. That's already three different perspectives that you can play around with. If you introduce more prepositions, you'll see how the object will shift in position. And it does not end there, what happens to the box is also another scenario that can affect the dynamics between the box and the object. Your task can be the object or the box. It's all up to you.

4. Combine different brainstorming techniques

A brainstorming technique that worked for other copywriters may not necessarily work for you. If this is the case, then it's time to tweak your technique and combine one or two or three techniques to get the best results. Because why not?

The more you are able to combine different techniques, the more powerful your brainstorming becomes. The deadly combination can have you thinking of ideas and creative ways to present your copy in no time. Of course, this is a trial and error kind of exercise, but it's one where you don't lose or suffer negative consequences. In fact, you'll emerge from the brainstorming with a clearer mind and a sharper focus. It's a win-win!

- Doing word associations is a good take-off point for building your word bank. The words you think of in relation to your project can be deposited to the word bank and you can withdraw it anytime you have a need for them.
- Visual associations can unearth tons of data and information. To make sense of all the information you have, you can try mind mapping to organize the associations and create a structure to which you can base your copy on—or at least draw inspiration from.
- When you're working with team members, you can brainstorm with a twist. For example, set a time limit for your brainstorming session. Once the time expires, you switch ideas with other members and you build on what they have started and vice versa. It forces everyone in the team to think differently because they are working on something that isn't their original idea. Your brains will be working overtime but it's guaranteed that you'll get interesting results. Remember, two heads are better than one.
- Forcing limits when you brainstorm can lead to quick decision-making. These limits can be in the form of time, resources, or both. One perfect example is the Rube Goldberg machine. It's a complex contraption designed to complete a simple task. You can apply this to brainstorming by limiting the time and the resources. For example, you need to think of 10 words that would describe the product but

they all must start with letter A. You're only given 3 minutes to do it and failure to do so would have repercussions.

Force limitation works because you are not paralyzed by too many options. You are forced to work within your limitations and the solution you think of is the best solution because other options have already been eliminated for you.

Tone of Voice

The way you deliver your message to your audience factors in the overall success of your copy and the marketing campaign. Writers have a way with words. They can weave sentences on the fly and tailor-fit the tone and style depending on the copy requirements. But there will be times when they go off-script and write for themselves and not for the reader.

Always remember that you are writing with a specific audience in mind. You write to persuade so you have to be clear about your message. You have to structure your copy in such a way that it could be understood by everyone who reads it.

If your message is clear, they would know what your product is all about, how it will solve their problem, and where they would go to complete their purchase journey.

Here's how:
- Write for your target audience

Remember the personas you created? Start from there. You know their needs and their problems. Craft your copy to let them know that you have the solution. Tell them that they will stand to benefit from the solution you are offering.

- Be a reliable problem-solver.

So, you dangle the solution to your customers' problem, but would they take the bait? If you provide them a reason to trust you, they probably would.

Some customers take little convincing. You just tell them the features and product and they're off to the checkout page. But some customers are not easily persuaded. They need more information and they want to know if you are trust-worthy. This is the part where you build trust with your audience by integrating testimonials, reviews, product ratings, press coverage, and case studies into your copy. These elements show people that you can back your claims with facts and can help remove doubts that they have about the product.

To further allay their fears, sweeten the deal with risk-free offers. Let them know that they can have a free trial for a certain period of time. You can also give them a money back guarantee offer so that it's zero-risk to them. Let them know that they are not pushed into a wall because they can cancel anytime if they are satisfied with the product.

It sends a message that you can be trusted.

- Get to the point.

Time is not on your side, so you better hook your web visitors in less than 10 seconds. While splashy animation and witty headlines may get their attention, they are not enough to make them stay. You have to present the features and benefits of the product in just a few seconds. Short and simple with flashes of creativity and cleverness will win visitors over. Imagine that you are writing for a school of goldfish with a very short 5-second attention span.

- Keep it conversational.

People can relate to things if you make your copy conversational. Using I, You, and We will get you far when it comes to connecting with potential customers. If you're too formal, your message would just go over their heads. Your audience doesn't care much about your jargons; they care about the solution you are offering them.

By having a conversational tone, you are encouraging them to interact. If you ask them questions, they're more likely to answer. Their participation is a barometer of how interested they are in the product.

- Show the brand's personality.

How a copy is written says so much about a brand's personality. Customers are more likely to develop an interest in your brand has the characteristics that your target consumer segment enjoys and loves. It's important to be consistent when presenting your brand's personality. For example, you can't be rugged in some of your copy and be sophisticated in others.

Brand personality not only sets you apart from the competition, but it also enables your message to resonate to the right customer segment.

- Use short concise sentences.

People relate to short simple words because that's how everyday language is. They want something that's personal and you can achieve this by talking to them using "I", "you", or "we". You must also use active voice instead of passive voice.

The structure of sentences in an active voice starts with the subject, followed by the verb, and then the object. This gives your writing a more vibrant and dynamic feel that easily engages your audience. The content is much easier to understand when there are fewer words. Brevity counts a lot when writing for the web.

Proven Formulas

Here's one trade secret that smart copywriters swear by: "Don't' start from scratch!" The trouble with starting from scratch is that it gives a lot of room for guesswork. If you don't know what you're doing, you'd end up second-guessing and third-guessing yourself and that doubt will show in your copy.

You're probably thinking that this advice goes against the "thinking out of the box" approach. Well, no. It just means that there are time-tested and proven formulas to make your copy even better. These formulas eliminate the guesswork, so you can focus on the meaty part of your copy. You're not reinventing the wheel. Why waste time figuring things out when it has already been figured out for you by someone else a long time ago? What you need to do is utilize these proven formulas, give it some flashes of your brilliance and sprinkle it with relevance and persuasion.

AIDA

AIDA stands for Attention, Interest, Desire, and Action. AIDA has been around since the 1900s, making it the oldest copywriting formula known to man. The fact that it is still being used to this day says so much about its effectiveness in presenting product benefits.

- **Attention** – To get your reader's attention, start with a bold headline—something that will wake them up from a deep slumber.
- **Interest** – Once you get the reader's attention, remind them about their pain points. Let them know that you hold the solution to their problems. Don't give them time to cast doubt on your bold claims. Show them that you have the answer to their nagging question: So what?
- **Desire** – When you have convinced them that your product is the real deal, you must hook them with your emotional benefits. Tug at their heartstrings and by appealing to their ambitions and aspirations. Show further proof to make them desire the product.
- **Action** – This is the part when the customer says, "Here, take my money! Take me to your leader!" (or something to that effect). You then guide the customer to the purchasing part of the journey by redirecting them to your ecommerce site to complete their purchase.

PAS

PAS stands for Problem, Agitate, Solution. While AIDA appeals to the customers' hopes and dreams, PAS uses the power of the dark side to remind customers that their fears and nightmares could materialize if they ignore the problem.

This is how PAS operates:

- **Problem** – Open your pitch with a problem, specifically your customer persona's biggest pain point. This is your selling point. When people are presented with a problem, they will do anything to avoid the pain, the hassle, and the inconvenience.
- **Agitate** – Amplify that problem by using power words that trigger fear and anger. Make them feel a little more uncomfortable by rocking the boat close to the tipping point.
- **Solution** – Present the solution to prevent their worst fears from happening. Show them that there is still a way out but they need to take one last step to ease their weary minds. This is when you close the deal.

PAS is effective because it pokes at the fears of the customers but gives them assurance in the end.

Imagine how much more powerful your copy can be when AIDA and PAS work together.

Try creating sample copies for the new tablet in the previous exercises. Write one sample using the AIDA formula, one sample using the PAS formula, and one sample combining both.

You must keep in mind that AIDA and PAS are flexible formulas. They serve as blueprints to shape or structure your copy. Don't get caught up with structure, your message is still more important than how you present it.

The You Language

"People aren't interested in you, they're interested in themselves."
– Dale Carnegie

Your copy is intended for your target audience. You're not writing for yourself or for the business. Forget about what you want to hear. Forget about your problems and pain points. Instead, ask yourself these questions:

- What would they want to hear or read?

- Why should they listen to you?

- What's in it for them?

One way to approach this is through role reversal. Put yourself in the shoes of the consumer. As a consumer, how do you choose which content to pay attention to?

What would compel you to click on ads or read posts on social media? Of course, the answers vary across consumer segments, but there are ways to get the general pulse of your target audience. You can do a research study or conduct an online survey to find out.

However, even if you have not done some research, you can still determine which type of content (or ads) appeal to the consumers.

Take this scenario:

Let's say you're visiting New York for the first time. You've heard about how great the pizzas are in the city. You have collected a list of the best pizzerias in the city. It would be impractical to visit them all and try all their pizzas, so you go to Yelp.com for recommendations. You read the reviews and you narrowed your list down to two pizzerias. You checked out their websites and saw their profile and pitch:

Pizzeria 1:

We're one of New York's finest Italian restaurants, offering the best pizzas in town. Our award-winning dishes are tightly-guarded family recipes passed down from generation to generation. Visit us for authentic Italian cuisine. We look forward to welcoming you into our home!

Pizzeria 2:

Are you searching for the best pizza in town? Take a bite of our award-winning pizza dishes prepared the traditional Italian way. You'll get a taste of our family recipes handed down from generation to generation. One bite and you'll discover why we're one of New York's finest pizzerias! Come visit us, we're waiting for you!

Which one would you choose?

Both pizzerias are essentially saying the same thing, but Pizzeria 2 utilizes the YOU language. This makes them much more attuned to the consumers. Instead of focusing on the business, Pizzeria 2 cared more for the consumers' pizza experience. In this aspect, Pizzeria 2 is much more effective. Whether their pizza tastes better than Pizzeria 1 is besides the point.

By using the YOU language, you are building an instant connection with your readers and potential customers. Customer-centric content gives the impression that you care about the customers.

Drill #4

Here's an example of the copy written for the "About Us" section of a company offering web development services:

We believe that every business, big or small, deserves an online presence. Our goal is to lower the technical and financial barriers that prevent businesses from making their own websites or online stores. We believe in combining innovation, creativity, and simplicity. We can't wait to help you on your journey!

Your mission, should you choose to accept it, is tweak the copy and use the YOU language to make it more relatable to the target audience. Make it about your customers to build a better connection.

Coffee Talks

Here's a technique that is so effortless and yet so effective: Talk to your customers as if you're chatting with a friend in a coffee shop.

Here's a scenario:

You're at your fancy neighborhood café, enjoying a cup of coffee and settling in to start working on your copy. Suddenly, you see a familiar face walk by. It's your friend you haven't seen in a long time. You invite her over and catch up on each other's lives.

The conversation went something like this:

Friend: What are you up to? What are you working on?

You: We're launching a new tablet next month.

Friend: Oh cool, tell me more about it!

Here's an opportunity for you to low-key promote the tablet. How would you answer your friend? What would your conversation be like? Go back to Drill #2. Transform the technical specs of the tablet into solutions that your friend could understand. If you can convince her that the tablet is the answer to a problem, then you're doing things right!

Write Like You Speak

Before social media exploded, the language used in business is formal, technical, and boring. The main goal is to inform about the product, what it can d, and why consumers should buy it. That's now a thing of the past.

Businesses, nowadays, are learning to become more accessible, sociable, personable, and relatable. The wall that separates brands and customers has been broken. They are now perceived as equals. And just like two old friends, they can communicate in an informal manner. This is why conversational writing is becoming more popular in the marketing and advertising space.

Conversational writing is essentially writing like you are speaking to a friend. There's less technical mumbo-jumbo and more excitement about the produce. You talk about the best features and how you'd fall in line or camp out the store just to get your hands on the product.

In copywriting, do the same thing. Highlight the features, preach about the benefits, and capture the excitement. Let your audience know that it's something that they needed in their life and they must have it.

If you're used to writing in a serious manner, switching to casual and conversational writing can be a challenge. But when you get the hang of it, you'll find that it's really enjoyable and you might not even want to go back to traditional business writing.

Here's how:

- **Write for one person:**
  Even if your copy reaches thousands of people, you only have to write for one person. Every person who reads the content would feel that the copy is addressed to them and no one else.

- **Keep it short and simple:**
  Use words that you normally use in conversations. Big words will only make your copy sound pretentious. Write the way you speak and people will get the message fast.

- **Keep it two-way:**
  Your copy should mimic a conversation. Even though you would not hear the readers' response, you know that they are responding when you ask them questions. This approach also helps you avoid switching the focus back to the company. Consumers tend to be more engaged when they are explicitly asked to be involved.

- **Use contractions:**
  Conversations are not academic papers. So, you have the permission of the grammar gods to use contractions like you're, aren't let's, we've, and

other combinations. By using contractions, your copy would flow better.

To check the overall tone and flow of your copy, read it to your friend. If she thinks it sounds natural, friendly, and non-salesy, then your job is done.

Drill #5

Let's go back to the coffee shop scene. How would you tell your friend about this new tablet that your client will launch next month? Start writing.

Think about their possible follow-up questions and continue writing. See where your conversation takes you.

Conversations Lead to Conversions

Have you ever listened to a sales guy talk about a product and it turned into a litany of technical specs? Yes? Don't be that guy. If you write the way that sales guy speaks, then it's no different from reading the technical specifications in the manual.

Writing a copy should be as easy as having a conversation. It should not be an aggressive sales pitch. People are put off by salesy copy. Remember, consumers have evolved and they don't want to be sold to. They wanted brands to treat them less as anonymous recipients and more as brand ambassadors.

Conversational writing makes your copy genuine and personal and more likely to engage the reader. It builds in building rapport with your target audience and may even hook consumers outside of your target demographics. These days, anything is possible because of social media's wider reach.

Even in long formats like an eBook, it helps to make your content easier to absorb and understand. Jargony content can alienate even your most loyal followers.

So, when in doubt, just pretend you're in a coffee shop talking to a friend about your product. Better yet, invite a real friend to a real coffee shop and see how the conversation goes and how you can use elements of it in your copy. Think of it as research. You'll be surprised at the things you'd discover.

Go on, put your new-learned skill to the test.

The Power of Words

Words have the power to persuade. It can change your relationship with your target audience. When used strategically, it can have a profound impact on your customers.

In copywriting, words have the ability to spark different emotions. You want your customers to feel a certain way. Whatever emotions that may be, they must lead to the end goal: to close a deal.

To know what words to use, you must first identify what your customers really care about. Go back to the personas you've created. What are their dreams and aspirations? What are the things they value the most? Fame? Money? Health? Security? Power? It's your job to figure this out and when you do, you can shape the content of your copy to make them feel a certain way.

Your copy must not only excite and intrigue your customers, but it must also evoke a genuine feeling of satisfaction, pleasure, and joy.

Seven Saleable Emotions

If you want your copy to be more compelling, you must trigger seven of the most saleable emotions. These are the buttons you need to push to make a compelling emotional impact.

- **Fear** – Fear is a powerful emotion that can compel people to buy a product. Products that offer safety, security, and peace of mind use fear to push their products to consumers. Just look at the copy for security cameras, car alarm system, locks, and vaults. How many times have you agreed to do or buy something simply out of fear?

- **Encouragement** – There are times when we feel that we need a boost of encouragement or confidence. The challenges we face can be too overwhelming that they make us doubt our skills and abilities. Words that trigger encouragement can help remove all these doubts.

- **Anger** – Some people respond better to a copy that echoes their anger and frustration. They are enraged that they could not find a solution to their problem.

- **Curiosity / Secrecy** – The element of intrigue will always get people's attention. Feed your customers' curiosity to hook and reel them in. It would be hard to resist a click.

- **Safety / Security** – The biggest challenge is gaining the trust of your customers. Remove their doubts by assuring them that the business is trustworthy and what you say about your product is true.

- **Lust –Sex sells.** Any product can be sexy in the hands of a good copywriter. Words can seduce the consumers into buying a product.

- **Greed** – Gordon Gecko said it best: Greed is right, greed works. This is why products that promise more money, bigger profits, and best results still sell like crazy. Even though they are overused, they are still effective.

So, which of these buttons would you like to push?

A Compelling CTA

What is a Call to Action?

A Call to Action (CTA) is a statement or a request designed to get a response from the reader of the copy. It's meant to prompt the customer on what to do next to complete the customer journey, which ultimately leads to the purchase of the product or service.

Many businesses make the mistake of assuming that if customers visit the ecommerce site, they would automatically buy product on offer or sign up to your newsletter, or whatever else you expect them to. After all, why would they be there in the first place?

Right?

Wrong!

Your readers are bombarded with exciting offers every single day. Even if you think your product is special, it may not be enough for the visitors to click on that magic button that would convert engagement to actual sales.

CTA will guide your customers to the right path and prevent them from clicking on something else. Sometimes, all they need is a little nudge to remind them that they need to close the deal.

Examples of Call to Action Words and Phrases

- ✓ Buy
- ✓ Call
- ✓ Click here for
- ✓ Donate
- ✓ Download
- ✓ Follow
- ✓ Order
- ✓ Register
- ✓ Share
- ✓ Sign-Up
- ✓ Subscribe

How to Write an Effective Call to Action (CTA)

The simple examples listed above work well, but that doesn't mean you can't explore other styles and methods. As they say, the best CTA method is the one that works!

Here are the best practices that can guide you in writing an effective CTA.

- **Know your desired outcome.**
  What is your desired result? A CTA must fit other parts or your marketing strategy. It can be an initial goal or the end goal. For example, you probably want to build a mailing list first before you get to the next phase of your marketing campaign. If this is the initial goal, then your CTA should be something like "sign up and get a free trial".

- **Keep it short and simple.**
  CTAs work best when they are direct to the point. There's no need to complicate it by making your visitors jump through hoops just to get to where they need to go. Don't give them multiple options. It slows down their decision-making. They just need to know where to click.

- **Bring on the benefit**
  You can add the emotional benefit to make your CTA connect with the target audience. The customer will ask himself "What's in it for me if I click on this button?" Make an offer they can't refuse—and that's usually something that benefits them. Clearly state what they will get by responding. You can offer them free reports, free trial, shopping vouchers, be part of an exclusive group, etc.

- **Use power words**
  These are words that are scientifically-proven to compel customers to action. By combining power words and benefits, you are putting them in a position to react in a positive way to what you are offering.

- **Sound urgent**
  CTAs with a limited time offer or a limited number of items gives a sense of urgency. This is where the Fear of Missing Out (FOMO) phenomenon kicks in. People don't want to miss out on something because they want to be part of something exclusive or something that may turn out to be big in the future.

These phrases should do the trick:

Free gift to the first 100 people to sign up
Sign-up now before someone steals your spot
Buy now while we still have this epic shirt in your size!

- **Remove the risks** – First-time visitors to your site will not automatically trust you. Even if they really want to buy your product, they will be hesitant to do so because of trust issues. In this case, your CTA must eliminate the risk by adding a risk-free clause with your offer:

Sign-up now for your free 30-day trial.
Subscribe now and cancel anytime.
Not satisfied? Get your money back. No questions asked.
No credit card needed

- **Track Your Results** – Not all CTA strategies would give the desired outcome. Some may work well, while others would be a complete bust. Tracking your results is necessary to test your different options. You can determine which phrases deter customers and which ones work like a charm.

Drill #6

Write 10 creative calls to action that relate to the new tablet that will be launched. Explore different styles and combinations of power words to make your CTA work for you.

Remember, the ultimate goal of any sales copy is conversion – and a compelling call to action is the last piece of the puzzle your readers need to complete their purchase journey.

Now jump to the next chapter to discover more secrets of killer copywriting, before others beat you to it!

Chapter 4 Branding with Words

USP and Tagline

USP

Unique Selling Proposition (USP) is what sets you apart from your competitors. It makes your brand or product highly desirable in the eyes of the consumers. It's your brand's edge and competitive advantage.

A marketing strategy or a marketing campaign is built around a brand's USP. All marketing collaterals are produced based on the USP—web content, keywords, landing pages, and every ad used in the promotion of the brand.

Every business must have a clear USP if it wants to be successful. Unfortunately, many businesses don't know what their USP is, much less what it means. However, they know why their customers keep coming back to do business with them. They are also aware of their competitor's strengths and weaknesses. From the data and information they have, businesses can formulate their USP.

Why is USP important?

- **USP differentiates you from your competitor.**
  A customer who is looking to buy flowers online will do a Google search and will find a list of competitor sites. Many of them offer the same products and services at the same price point. If your online flower shop is the only shop that

offers free same-day delivery, then the customer will buy from your site and not from your competitor.

- **USP prevents you from engaging in price wars.**
  Lowest price is a legitimate USP. Consumers love price wars because they benefit from the price drop. For companies, price wars lower their profit margins. If you have a product that has a USP, you don't have to lower your price just to compete with others. If you operate in a small market, price wars are likely to happen. However, if you know that you have an edge because of the quality and features of your product, you don't have to lower your price.

What does a USP look like?

A common misconception is that USP is the same as a tagline. They are not the same. A USP encapsulates what makes your product unique and desirable to consumers. It can be presented in just a few words or it can be an entire paragraph.

Ask yourself this: Why should a potential customer buy from you and not from your competitor?

If you can answer that question, you have yourself a USP that will be the cornerstone of your marketing endeavors.

Examples of Successful USPs

✓ Southwest Airlines: We are the low-fare airline

✓ Domino's: Pizza delivered in 30 minutes or it's free.

✓ Woolworths: The Fresh Food People

✓ M&M's: The milk chocolate melts in your mouth not in your hand.

✓ Dropbox: Dropbox keeps your files safe, synced, and easy to share. Bring your photos, docs, and videos anywhere and never lose a file again.

How to write USP that sells

1. Choose the category of your USP.

Convenience
Customization
Guarantee
Originality
Price
Quality
Selection
Service
Specialization
Speed

2. Identify your strengths.

These questions will guide you:
  ✓ What do you offer that the competitor can't deliver?
  ✓ Why do customers keep coming back to you?
  ✓ Is your product easy for the competitors to copy?

✓ How easy is it to communicate your
product's unique offering?
3. Flesh out ideas and concepts

The answers you have in #2 are most likely general
ideas and broad concepts. You have to go to the
specifics. You can't just say your service is great or
your product is the best. You have to explain why they
are the best or why they are great.

4. Show Proof.
You have to back up your claims with proof.
Testimonials, reviews, and endorsements are your
social proof points.

Taglines

A tagline is a short phrase or sentence that represents
the brand's philosophy. It's written to be clever, fun,
and memorable so that it has a high memory recall.
Successful taglines connect the product with their
target audience. They encapsulate the business in just
a few words.

Here are some of the legendary taglines that stood the
test of time:

✓ Just Do It. (Nike, 1988)
✓ Have A Break. Have a Kit Kat. (Rowntree,
1957)
✓ Finger Lickin' Good (KFC, 1952)
✓ Where's the Beef? (Wendy's, 1984)
✓ Got Milk? (California Milk Processor Board,
1993)
✓ Impossible is Nothing (Adidas, 2004)

- ✓ It's The Real Thing (Coca-Cola, 1970)
- ✓ Once You Pop, You Can't Stop (Pringles, 1990)
- ✓ The Best A Man Can Get (Gillette, 1989)
- ✓ Think Different (Apple, 1990s)
- ✓ When You Care Enough to Send the Very Best (Hallmark, 1934)

Types of Taglines

- Taglines that ask questions. These taglines make people think and establish desire.
- Taglines that make statements. They tell people what to think about the product.
- Taglines that explicitly communicate a benefit. They tell consumers that they have a solution to a problem.

How to develop a tagline

1. **Keep it simple.**
   A tagline should not be complicated. It's not a puzzle that needs to be solved.
2. **Get to the point.**
   You only have a few words to work with, you can't afford to beat around the bush.
3. **Tell a story in just a few words.**
   It will resonate with consumers because they will get the context.
4. **Bring on the Benefits.**
   People care more about the benefits than the features. If the tagline highlights the benefits, they are more likely to respond to it in a positive way.

Website Content

Writing content for a website or a web page has a different set of nuances. You can't just copy the content you wrote for a broadsheet and post it online and expect massive web traffic. The truth is that what you publish offline don't always translate well online.

Web content is a different beast with an extremely finicky audience. If you don't get their attention in the first 10 seconds of reading your copy, they're gone. They will be more than happy to click on the next shiny link with a click-baity headline.They consume content so fast that their decision-making is just as quick. You have to make your point before their attention shifts somewhere else.

Main Tasks
If your client asks you to write for a website, he or she is telling you to write for:
- An online store (e-commerce)
- A full corporate site (company)
- A landing page (individual or business)

These are the three main types of a web page you're likely to work with if you are tasked to do website content. Of course, there are subtypes that can branch out or even overlap with other types of content. But for now, we're sticking to these three.

A company website largely has a static content laced with corporate-speak and jargons that people don't really care much for. However, it doesn't mean you can't put a call to action. When a company has social media accounts, it's less likely that customers would search for the corporate website if they want to get updates. While a corporate website may just be an afterthought, it's not useless—not all. It can still be used to acquire leads from newsletter signups and divert traffic to the company's social media accounts For an online store or e-commerce, you need to be concise about the information you want to communicate. Your audience will not stick around to read long text. So, you have to get straight to the key features and benefits and lock them in.

You must write in as few words as you can possibly write without losing the main message. You're not only writing brochures, but you're also building a complete catalog of products or services. Leave the technical stuff to the IT guys and you're really left with a mountain of copywriting to do.Your work doesn't stop when you're done describing the products' features. You have to be cognizant of the fact that your potential customers can change their minds midway through the buying process. Even if they have already added items in their shopping cart, there's always that small window for doubt.

When writing, you must factor in that doubt and reassure customers that they are making the right purchasing decision by buying the product that you are promoting. A landing page is similar to a sales letter in many ways. They have an old-school letter vibe to it, but the words are extra bold, confident, and persuasive. You're still making a direct appeal to the visitor of the page, but the choice of words is updated and relevant.

What do you want to achieve?

Web content covers a lot of ground, so you have to ask yourself what is the goal you want to achieve. You may have to work closely with a web designer if you want to know if a particular content will translate well online.

When writing for the web, you have to wear several hats. It's not just about wording something in a certain way or using the right words; you have to know the medium you are using inside out. Writing for the web is so dynamic and it offers a lot of avenues to be creative. It is alive with unlimited possibilities and it's your job to harness the power of the medium and use it to the company's advantage.

Here's a list of what you can do:
- Sell products
- Offer services
- Promote a business
- Invite people to sign up for newsletters
- Sign up new clients
- Get people to support a political candidate
- Create awareness about a charity program
- Provide a demo of how a product works
- Promote a lifestyle
- Build a community of people with similar interests
- Launch a new product
- Get information from customers
- Persuade angel investors that your startup is worth investing in
- Get people to apply for a job
- Get employers to post a job on the site
- Ask people to advertise on the site
- Act as a forum to interact and exchange ideas

This is just some of the things you can do when writing for the web. You can do one or a combination of them, but it has to be aligned to the goals of the company.

Strengths and Weaknesses

To know how to write effectively for the web, you must first know the medium's strengths and weaknesses. You have to know its quirks and nuances so you can write the content that would harness the strengths and downplay the weaknesses.

Strengths

As a communications medium, the web is effective in providing the information that people are searching for. Everything they need they can find on the web and they are comfortable using it in their day-to-day lives. They use it pretty much for everything that it becomes a necessary part of their lives. This high dependence on the web is an opportunity that must not be wasted.

Another strength of the web as a medium is the flexibility to which content can be changed as marketing goals change. There's almost no time lag when you need to change your copy. This enables companies to adjust their marketing strategies when certain aspects of the marketing campaign fail to deliver the desired results. This means you can also change your message on the fly. It's all possible to make mid-course corrections and adjustments so even if the first phase fails, the campaign can still succeed in the endgame.

The relatively cheaper cost to launch a website is another strength of the web. That's why companies are building their e-commerce websites to establish their online presence and position their brands to succeed.

Weaknesses

The common misconception about building a website is that if you build it, they will come. This is not always true. In fact, it is not true most of the time. Unless there is a serious effort to push the website to social media platforms and other communication channels, don't expect people to flock to your site.

What's closer to reality is: "If you promote it, they will come". This means pulling no stops—spending on ads and optimizing the site so that it would have more visibility in search engines.

Granting that you have already lured audiences to your site, does the site have enough hold on them to make them stick around long enough to buy your product, sign up to your mailing list, share your posts, or respond to your call to action?

The biggest disadvantage of the medium is that it's easy for people to abandon websites when they don't find what they're looking for. They don't feel the same connection they have when they can touch or interact with the product. And if the website is hard to navigate, people simply disengage.

What you should not do:
- **Don't just copy your offline copywriting and paste it onto your website**

Even if your offline copywriting is brilliant and critically acclaimed, it doesn't mean it would get the same reception online. You have to write from a web content perspective. You have only a few seconds to hook them so your copy must straight to the point with a sense of extreme urgency.

- **Don't use long baggy sentences**

Online, you do not have the luxury of time. You have to explain things as succinctly as possible using fewer words. If you found using more than 12 words in a sentence, you are doing it wrong.

- **Avoid using an impersonal or a pompous tone of voice**

If you start your copy with phrases that sound pompous and pretentious, you create a separation between the company and the audience. The arrogant tone can drive your customers away. You can be professional without sounding superior to your audience. Remember, you want to reel them in, not turn them away.

Avoid the following phrases if you can!
"It goes without saying…"
"Let me be perfectly clear…"
"With all due respect…"
"We at ABC Corporation…"
"Not to mention…"

- Avoid link overload

One SEO strategy is to create backlinks to your previous articles within the website so that you can keep your visitors longer. The more they linger in the website, the higher the chance that they'd respond to your call of action positively. In an e-commerce site, you want to guide your visitors to their purchase journey. You want them to stay with you as you reveal your story. If you hyperlink every other phrase, you run the risk of losing your visitors before you can even deliver your pitch. They might not even finish reading your article because your links are driving them away. Find a healthy balance between SEO tactics and copywriting good practices.

- **Stop keyword stuffing**

Google punishes those who practice keyword stuffing. What is keyword stuffing, anyway? It is the bad practice of loading your web pages with keywords with the intention of manipulating the website's ranking in search results.

There's no harm in adding a healthy number of keywords, but just don't overdo it. If you pepper your content with keywords it can give a negative experience to your site visitors.

It's easy to recognize keyword stuffing because the sentences are repetitive and don't add value to the content. But more than that, it would read like it was written by article spinners. And that's a no-no! It not only sounds unnatural and unprofessional, but it also makes you look bad as the copywriter.

For example:
We sell custom dog tag collars. Our custom dog tag collars are handmade and use high-quality materials. If you want to order our dog tag collars, please contact our dog tag collar specialists at dogtagcollars@dogtagcollars.com

Can anything be more annoying than that?

Over-optimizing your content is counter-productive. It defeats the purpose of your SEO efforts. But more than that, it is a visitor repellant. People would not want to read your articles because it is unprofessionally and poorly written.

What You Must Include
Here's what you must include in your content whether you're writing for an e-commerce site, a corporate site, or a landing page.

- ✓ **For an e-commerce page:**
    - ○ Features and benefits
    - ○ Size and dimension
    - ○ Price
    - ○ Testimonials

- o Call to Action button or text

- ✓ **For a landing page:**
  - o Features and benefits
  - o Pictures of the product with caption
  - o Solution to the problem
  - o Testimonials from satisfied customers
  - o Call to action button or text

- ✓ **For a corporate website:**
  - o Product information
  - o Case studies
  - o Testimonials from customers
  - o Testimonials from employees
  - o Company history
  - o Qualifications and experience to offer the product or service to the customer
  - o Contact information
  - o Social media badges and links

The list is by no means exhaustive, but they are the things that you must include. You can leave out other inessential things because they just clutter up the content.

Web Content Formatting Best Practices

People consume online content differently than they do print copy. When they are visiting websites, they are actively searching for something. Unlike in print materials where users just accept the information presented to them, in websites, the users search for information.

Since there is a massive amount of content online, users just quickly scan the content to find the information they are looking for. If they don't find it immediately, they move on to the next content. They keep scanning information at a quick pace until they find what they're looking for.

Knowing this user behavior can help you structure your copy so that it would align with the needs of the content users. There really are no hard and fast rules about content format or structure because they change rather quickly. However, there are best practices that you can follow to help shape your copy to be optimized for online consumption.

- Create scannable text.

When you write for the web, you must break up the content in easily digestible text. This makes it easier for users to pick out individual words or phrases.

Here's how you can convert your content to scannable text:

✓ Use headings and subheadings
✓ Use bulleted lists
✓ Highlight keywords
✓ Use one idea per paragraph
✓ Use short paragraphs (3-4 sentences)
✓ Use short sentences (12 words or less)

- Create a scent of information for users to follow.

As soon as users arrive at a web page, they are on the hunt for information. They go through an enormous amount of content but they only scan them. If they don't find what they're looking for, they move to the next. The question is how do they choose the next link to click? The answer is by virtually sniffing out a scent of information. The link that has the strongest scent is most likely the next destination.

So, how do you create a stronger scent of information?

- ✓ Place important information and links on the upper part of the webpage, so even if the user does not scroll down to the lower part of the page, they wouldn't be overlooking important information.

- ✓ Use inline links. This means that links should be in the body of the copy appearing in blue text with an underline. Avoid making links appear as images because they have a high chance of being overlooked. Don't camouflage your links.

- ✓ Don't place your links near banner ads or filler content because users tend to ignore that area of the web page.

- ✓ Don't use misleading links. Make sure that the linked words or phrases would lead to a webpage with relevant content; otherwise, users would lose confidence in the information and abandon the scent altogether.

- ✓ Make links clear and explicit. Avoid using cute or playful link names that don't align with the context of the content. Users will find them suspicious and avoid them like the plague.

- ✓ Use links as cues that will guide users to the information they need. Keep them within the pages of the site until they find the information that they are looking for.

- Create links to your call to action and conversion pages. Use cues like click here, sign up today, download now, and other that would take visitors to your goal.

A Word About Keyword
The importance of keywords in web content writing cannot be overemphasized. Keywords are essentially the search words, terms, or phrases that people use to find what they're looking for in the web—it could be a business, a product, an event, or pretty much anything.
Keyword is the language that search engine crawlers understand.

Google and other search engines can only make sense of your content because of keywords. Without keywords, they would not be able to rank your page. That's why it's an absolute must to skillfully weave the keywords into your copy to boost the chance of being understood by the search engine algorithm.

And that's the oversimplified explanation of search engine optimization or SEO. Of course, there is a whole gamut of important factors to consider in order for your web pages to rank in the search, but keywords remain relevant in getting more traffic to your web page.

Knowing how keywords play a role in search engine ranking, people have found a way to outsmart the algorithms by keyword stuffing. It reached a point where the content doesn't make sense anymore; they're just a wall of text filled with keywords.

Fortunately, the search engines penalized those who try to game the system. Let this be your word of caution not to fill your copy with keywords. Integrate your target keywords seamlessly and make sure they fit in the conversation.

Rule of thumb:
Write for your readers first, and Google second.
If you provide valuable content and solution to your customers, website optimization and conversion will follow.

Case Studies

Case studies are a great way to convert your audience into an actual paying customer. If you're not using them as part of your marketing campaign, you are missing out on the opportunity to persuade your audience to trust and try your product.

Don't be intimidated by the term case study. It's not some elaborate scientific experiment that you have to do. Essentially, a case study is a story that showcases how you have helped a customer solve a problem. It demonstrates the actual benefit that your customer gained from using your product or service.

Case studies are synonymous to customer success stories. It's just really a story of a happy and satisfied customer that you would use to get the attention of the people who are struggling to find a legitimate solution to the same problem. And what better way to persuade them than to show proof?

Case studies have their beginnings in business schools where real world business problems are identified, studied, and assessed in the hope of finding solutions. Case studies with successful outcomes are then used as "best practice" or blueprints being followed by businesses who want to replicate the success.

In the realm of copywriting, case studies show your target audience that you are an expert or an authority in what you do—and that's some pull if you want to influence people's purchasing decisions.

Why Case Studies Work?

- Case studies are factual. They are loaded with facts so there's no need to embellish the truth.
- Case studies are less about sales and more about information dissemination. They highlight the features and showcase the benefits.
- With case studies, other people are involved. The information did not just come from you (as a writer), but from different users of the product or service.
- Case studies help build trust with the target audience. When trust is there, they become less skeptical of your offer.

What can you use case studies for?

Although case studies are effective marketing content, they are not for everyone. They are mostly suited for more sophisticated products and services. If you sell phones or gadgets, a case study is not necessary. But if you are offering a service where a good reputation is required, then a case study will help in building and highlighting that reputation.

Case studies would be beneficial if you are writing a copy to promote any of the following products or services:

✓ Advertising
✓ Coaching (Business or Executive)
✓ Industrial plant manufacture
✓ Information Technology provider
✓ Law firms
✓ Management consultancy
✓ Management training
✓ Marketing agency
✓ Media
✓ PR consultancy
✓ Property development
✓ Scientific services for industry

Get Started
   ## 1. Find the right person or business to feature in the case study.

Finding someone to become the "face" of your case study requires research and sorting through all the feedback about your product. There will good and bad criticisms and they are both important, but for a case study, you'd want to find someone who has a positive experience using your product.

Here are ways you can start:

- Go through your social media accounts and see who said something positive about your product.
- Check out external reviews sites and read the good reviews. You can create a list and you can narrow it down based on a set of criteria (more on this below).
- Check in with your technical support team or customer support representatives, especially those who are assigned in after-sales support. They can provide you information on users who have nice things to say about the product.

The ideal case study subjects are people who:
- ✓ Use your products to solve their problems
- ✓ Love the company and understand your product
- ✓ Share their good experience in using your product

2. Track your business data using metrics and analytics.

This may sound complex, but it's really just having a way to track the performance of your products. If the products meet or exceed the success criteria and benchmarks that the company has set out, then it means the product is performing well. You can build your case study around that success.

3. Select from a shortlist of candidates.

There will probably a huge list of happy customers who use your product but you have to choose one that meets the following criteria:
- ✓ A customer who's recognizable in social media. You want someone who also has a good reputation. This is important because the customer would indirectly be representing the product and the brand once you launch the case study.
- ✓ A customer who has clout. It's not necessary that the customer be a famous social media influencer or a celebrity. He or she just has to be able to sway people into trying your product. A little bit of online presence and influence can do wonders but it's the customer's testimonial that has more weight.

✓ A customer who represents the typical customer in the business area you want your products to succeed.

4. Approach the chosen ones.
If you have chosen the best fit for your case study, you can reach out to them through email to make more formal than just sliding in their private messages in social media.

Let them know why you want to feature them in your case study, how they will benefit from the collaboration, how it will be done. You must also inform them when the case study would be published.

It is also important to include a case study release form in the email so that both parties would be clear about internal and legal clearances before the case study could proceed.

Questions to Ask

It's important to give the participant case study interview question well in advance so that they can have enough time to go over each question. If they know beforehand what to expect, they will be better prepared to answer the questions—regardless if the interview would be done in person or through email.

- What is your business?
- What products and services do you use in your business operations?
- How long have you been using the products and services?

- What specific problems and challenges were you experiencing before you use or products and services?
- What made you choose our products and services over the others?
- In what way did our products help your business?
- How did you achieve your desired outcome?
- Did you encounter any problems or challenges while using our products? How were you able to resolve them?
- What kind of results did you get? Do they match your desired outcomes? How do you feel about the results?
- What stood out for you when using the products/services?
- Would you recommend the product to other businesses?
- What would you tell someone who's not yet sold on the idea of what the product can do?

These are just the starter questions you can ask. It's much more preferable if you can have a chat online or in person to do the interview because the interview would be more conversational. You can ask follow-up questions on the fly.

You have to avoid asking questions that are answerable by "yes" or "no" because it will kill the interview and you will not get as much information as your case study requires.

If you plan on recording the interview, you have to ask for the participants' consent. You also have to inform them that you would use the recordings like video clips, audio, or transcript and share it in various media platforms.

What you must include in your case study?
The simple answer is to include as much information as you possibly can without duplication. The proof is in the details. Your case study would be persuasive if you back your claims with hard facts. This means showing statistics, figures, and any other quantifiable benefits.

No one can argue with you because the facts cannot be discredited.
But, of course, you still have to structure all the information in an easy-to-understand format. The following details must be included.

✓ Client's profile. This includes the client's name, the organization, job title, type of industry, and other information that will flesh out the client so that the readers can easily identify with the client. The more information you give about the client, the higher the chance you readers will find a connection or something in common.
✓ A detailed description of the problem that made the client come to you for help.
✓ A timeline of the process from problem identification to resolution. This is to show the reader to see the sequence of events that led to the desired outcomes.
✓ Detailed information about your organization, including experience, skills, products, services, technologies, processes, and other assets that you have that can help your clients.
✓ Detailed information about how the product or service works. This includes what exactly the people involved do to solve the problem.
✓ Details of how the project turned out. It is obvious that you are only going to include the

positive outcome. Highlight how the client was able to achieve the desired results because they used your product.

✓ Direct quotation from the client. This serves as the client's testimonial. They're essentially glowing remarks and high praises for the product.

The Structure

Headline:
This is the title of the client's success story. Don't make it sound like a sales pitch. Instead, encapsulate the problem or the challenge.

Subtitle:
This is the part where you tell the readers that the material is a case study.

Introduction:
This is where you tell the readers what the case study is about in outline. Don't give out details, just enough information to make them want to know more about the success story.

Section 1:
This describes the problem in detail. This includes how the problem led the client to see help and how the product helped put things right. The client is also introduced in this section.

Section 2:
This describes the client's journey to finding the product. It is also the perfect time to establish your organization's credibility, including the skills,

experience, awards, profitability, and other milestones.

Section 3:
This is where you explain what happened. Get into much detail as you want as long as you keep it interesting. Other people involved in the process can be introduced and show their involvement and in what capacity. You can include quotes from key players and make it appear that they are in a dialogue with the readers. It makes your narrative more interesting and engaging.

Section 4:
This is where you tell the readers the outcome. Let the readers know if the client got the desired benefits from using the product. Provide hard facts using statistics, figures, and other important metrics to quantify the product's contribution to the client's success.

Section 5:
This is the part where you tell the readers that the relationship does not end. You may suggest that the product can do more. It's a subtle way of saying that your organization would like to continue working with the client so that the success can be sustained in the long term. "Next Steps" and "Further Growth" can be used as headings to instill in the readers' minds that having a long-term relationship with your organization will be rewarded with future successes.

Final section:
This is where you make your pitch using call to action. Avoid making it sound like an aggressive sales pitch. Keep it subtle and friendly. Encourage your readers to respond to your call to action by giving them

incentives to do so. You must include all contact details so that the readers can get in touch with you from different channels. An example of an incentive would be a free 30-minute consultation, free trial of the product, or a free e-book.

Things to add to enhance the presentation of your case study
- ✓ Use a serious style and tone of voice
- ✓ Use actual images. Don't use stock photos because they don't have anything to do with the case study. Images must be taken from actual processes. Stock photos or library images give the impression that your story is not true and most likely fabricated.
- ✓ Direct quotations must be accompanied by photos of the people who said them.
- ✓ Use flowchart, tables, illustrations, graphs, and timelines to illustrate the processes. It makes complex processes easier to understand.

Press Releases

A press release is a subtle advertising material that's given free to media organizations, news teams and journalists. Although it's freely distributed, it's not guaranteed to make the news rounds. Journalists are not obligated to use your press release so don't expect them to use your material. They are extremely busy people that make decisions in a flash when it comes to choosing what stories to run or news to publish.

If your press release is boring and below par, it would get deleted. This is a lost opportunity on your part. Instead of journalists picking up your news and distributing to a wider audience for greater exposure, it's ignored forever.

Why send press releases?
Businesses and organizations have different reasons why the send press releases to the media channels.

- ✓ To get media exposure when your company releases a new product or a new feature for an existing product.
- ✓ To do damage control when the company is involved in a controversy. It's part of crisis management on the part of the company.
- ✓ To build or strengthen the brand's reputation. When media outlets pick up your press release, it gives the impression that the brand is reputable and trustworthy.
- ✓ To create an online or offline presence. It is a way to promote the company, organization, or the brand. It helps drum up interest in a product because of the media coverage.
- ✓ To increase online reputation through backlinks. This helps in the search engine optimization efforts of the organization.

When to send a press release

- ✓ Product launches. When the company is launching new products, a press release can help spread the word to a bigger audience.
- ✓ Breaking news or announcements. Media outlets want to be the first to cover breaking news.
- ✓ Research breakthroughs. When an organization launches a research study and discovers something new, it's worth writing a press release about.
- ✓ Events. Reporters usually cover important events especially when it involves famous

celebrities and influential personalities from across different industries.

✓ Company milestones. When a company reaches a milestone in its operations, a press release is warranted. This includes achieving sales goals or celebrating years of existence.

✓ Awards and accolades. When organizations are given awards, they want to shout it to the world. A press release will achieve this especially when reporters pick them up.

✓ Changes in the organization's management. When there is a change in the management or new executives join the organization, a press release is necessary, especially in listed companies.

✓ Partnerships. When organizations partner with other organizations, it's big news in certain industries because it affects the overall competition.

✓ Disasters, scandals, accidents, deaths. When something untoward happens to the organization, a press release is immediately sent to different news organizations to set things straight. This is done to stop speculations and shot down rumors.

What to include in your press release?

Like in any copywriting medium, you must plan how you will write your press release. The "Who? What? Where? When? Why? and How?" still work in the opening paragraph, but you have to make it sound interesting so that it will pique the interest of the journalist or the reporters. Plant something there that would make them curious and interested in covering.

Aside from the announcement or the story itself, a press release will have mandatory elements:

- ✓ The words "Press Release" on top
- ✓ Release date or embargo date: When there is an embargo, journalists cannot publish the information or news until a certain date or if certain conditions have been met.
- ✓ The word "End" or three centered #s to mark the end of the press release.
- ✓ Headline: This is the title of the announcement.
- ✓ Press Contact: Indicate the contact details of the person who can provide information if there are inquiries.
- ✓ City, State, Location
- ✓ Boiler Plate: This is a brief profile of the organization.
- ✓ Details of any photo opportunity.

Press Release Best Practices

- **Think like a journalist**

Do you know how an investigator catches a serial killer? He thinks like one. This is pretty much the same in the case of press releases. Your press release will not go straight to the audience. It has to go through the screening process of a journalist. So you're writing it to pitch a story to the journalist first, the readers second.

- ✓ Make important information easy to find. Get to the point. There's no room for unnecessary verbose writing.
- ✓ Keep the press release short. Journalists are some of the busiest people in the world. They receive tons of leads from several sources. They have no time to read your fluff.

✓ Avoid superlatives. Journalists know what the best events are or what the best products are, so if you oversell your press release, they will know.

- Send your press release to organizations whose audience would find value in your news or announcement

Avoid blindly sending press releases to everyone. There's no point in sending a press release about a mobile device to an organization that writes about car parts. That's an auto-delete.

✓ You must also know the readership of the news organization or media group you are trying to send the press release to. If their readership and your organization care about the same things, then by all means, send the press release.

✓ Your product or service must also align with the publication's coverage area. They would not waste time covering your news if your product is remotely related to the topics they cover.

- **Write in the third person.**

Instead of this:

"At ABC Ltd., we are pleased to announce..."

Write this:

"ABC Ltd. today announces it will build its second power plant..."

- **Include sound bites or quotes**

If you have quotes from an important person from the organization, you are making the journalist's job a lot easier. This is because they can just copy and paste it to their own articles.

- **Eliminate fluff**

If journalists have to wade through a wall of fluff, kiss your press release goodbye. They will not cover it for the simple reason that they could not find the point of your story in the opening paragraph.

- **Keep it as short as possible.**

Make your press release free of jargon and flowery language. They're unnecessary.

- **Keep the tone neutral.**

Avoid hype and overly enthusiastic writing. It has to be more in line with journalistic writing—dispassionate, informative, and neutral.

- **Use images**

If you make images available, journalists can just use them to accompany their articles. This will save them time instead of scheduling a photo-opportunity for them to take their pictures.

Just remember these:

✓ The images must be of high resolution so that it can be published on print.

✓ You must own the copyright to the images or you must have a license to use it.

✓ You must supply the caption for the images to let the journalists know what the photo is showing.

✓ Conclude with a few sentences that explain how the news links back to your organization. Highlight the company's skills and experience, but don't go overboard. Keep it factual and to the point. Remember, they can fact-check your claims and assertions.

Product Descriptions

It's easy to underestimate the power of product descriptions because when you see one, you think you've seen them all. Most production descriptions you read are heavy on technical specs. It will make you ask, so what?

That's the problem with many product descriptions you see on various ecommerce sites. Companies tend to let the photos sell their products. It may work a few times, but it may not be sustainable. If you don't use product description the way it should be used, you are losing sales opportunities.

What is Product Description?
Product description provides information about an item being sold. It describes the physical attributes of a product as well as the technical specifications, if any. It includes the features and benefits of a product. The goal is to compel customers to purchase the product immediately.

Before you write your product description, ask yourself these questions:
- ✓ That problem (pain points) does your product solve?
- ✓ What benefits does your customer gain from using your product?
- ✓ What separates your product from your competitors (unique selling points)?

Your production description must answer these important questions in a way that is easy for your customers to understand.

How to Write Product Descriptions That Sell

- **Focus on your buyer.**

Get to know your target audience. Always go back to the persona you have created which represents the ideal customer for your product. Imagine you are having a conversation with them over a cup of coffee. What's their personality and attitude? What makes them tick? What kind of question are they likely to ask you about the product? How would they react to your answers? Take that conversation to your website and apply it to your product descriptions.

- **Convert product features to benefits.**

As a copywriter, you must know the product inside out to capture the product features and present them in a well-written copy. But it doesn't end there. You have to translate these features into benefits. These are solutions to the customers' problems. Highlight the benefits and assure them that their problems and frustrations would be addressed by using the products.

- **Sell the experience.**

Salesy phrases such as superior quality or the best in its class might have worked three decades ago, but it would not have the same impact in today's competitive business market. They're basically a generic sales pitch with no real value.

You have to show customers that using the product will give them an extraordinary experience that makes their lives better. You can describe that the whitening toothpaste has a peppermint flavor that keeps your breath fresh for 24 hours, but what you're really selling is the experience of having pearly white teeth and minty fresh breath which can boost self-confidence. Sell not just the product, but the experience as well.

- **Support your claims.**

If you are going to describe the product using superlatives like biggest, fastest, strongest, or most effective, you better have the proof to support your claims. The features can back up the benefits, but the best proof is in the customer reviews and testimonials. Adding them on your product page with an image of the reviewer and a snippet of their review will give legitimacy to your claims.

- **Tease your customer's imagination.**

Selling online has its own set of challenges, one of which is the inability of the customers to see, touch, and test the product before purchase. They would have to rely on photos and product descriptions. If they don't trust you enough, they will not buy. But if you are truthful in your description and you utilize the power words and sensory words, you can create a copy that will tease the imagination of your customer. They can experience the product through the power of words.

Blog

Blog as a marketing platform has become more prevalent because there are now tools and resources that make publishing content on the web a whole lot easier. Even individuals with no technical experience can set up a blog in just a few minutes. From the consumer perspective, they are now bombarded with blog posts about pretty much any topic. Whether this is good or bad depends on how people make use of the blog.

How blogs are being used?
According to Statista, there are 31.7 million bloggers in the US alone. This translates to more than 25 billion pages viewed every month. What this means is that even with the rise of the social media platforms, blogging as a way to communicate is still a solid option.

Each blog has its own set of goals and objectives. Individuals and corporations use blogs to send messages to their respective audiences. Blogs fall into these overarching categories:

- ✓ Corporate Blogs
- ✓ Online Journal /Diary
- ✓ Hobbies or Interest Blogs
- ✓ Professional/Income Earning Blogs
- ✓ Community

Benefits of Blogging for Your Business
A company blog plays a huge role in any content marketing strategy. It presents an opportunity to establish the company as an industry expert. With high shareability on social media, your company can promote its product and brand to a wider audience.

Here are the powerful benefits of blogging:

1. **Boosts Search Engine Optimization Efforts:** By blogging consistently, you are providing fresh content that major search engines Google, Bing, and Yahoo love to crawl and index. With the proper use of keywords, blogs can help increase

the page ranking of not just the blog but also of the company website.

2. **Connects Consumers to Your Brand:**
   The more information you give out on your blog posts, the more people would be intrigued and interested in your products. Because blogs have a wider audience reach, you are effectively creating awareness about your brand.

3. **Strengthens Relationship with Existing Customers:**
   A relationship doesn't end after the purchase of a product. You have to maintain your relationships with your customers so that they will keep coming back. Aside from social media, a blog is a great platform to reach out to your customers to let them know the latest updates about the product.

4. **Gives More Business Clout in the Industry:**
   If you provide valuable expert information and content, you are not only educating the customers, you are also establishing the business as an expert in the industry.

5. **High Social Shareability:**
   Your blog posts have the potential to go viral if shared in social media platforms. Blogs are now designed for easy sharing. Your blog content can give your brand the exposure it needs in other platforms.

Best Practices for Company Blog

1. Before you launch your blog, determine what you want to achieve from creating the blog. Is it solely for SEO and organic search traffic? For social shares? To educate? To increase brand awareness? Whatever your goal, make sure that it is measurable so that you'll its impact on your profits.

2. Write Purposely. Blogging for the sake of having content is useless blogging. Your content must have a purpose. It must achieve something or it must provide value and benefit to the reader.
3. Blog Frequently. Fresh content is what you feed the search engines. The more quality content you produce, the more the search engines would be good to you.
4. Create an organized content calendar. It's not enough to just post content when you feel like it. You have to schedule your posts at strategic times so that you'll have maximum viewership. Posting three times a week is optimal. Add current events or real-time trending topics to make your post fresh and relevant.
5. Use videos and images. Walls of text are boring and can drive visitors away. Mix up your content to include videos and images. You can either embed the videos on your posts or provide a link from your YouTube channel.
6. Focus on establishing expertise. The most common mistake that businesses do is self-promotion in their blog posts. You should focus on adding value to your products and services to benefit the consumers. Your posts should provide insight into the industry, report about the latest technology, explain current business trends, and showcase the best practices in your industry. If you focus on selling, don't expect people to hang out in your blog. Remember, people don't like to be sold to.
7. Write long-form blog posts. If you're writing about what other bloggers have already written about, there's little value in your content. You have to go in-depth and write insightful content.
8. Update your top-performing blog posts. Your most visited blog post will likely rank high in

search engine results. It will likely generate more traffic for the blog even though it's an old content. To keep getting traffic, you should update it by adding relevant and current content.

9. Focus on quality, not quantity. There is really no evidence to suggest that more blog posts translate to more traffic and eventually sales. So, instead of being a prolific blogger writing only short posts, focus on in-depth articles that provide value to the readers.

Chapter 5 Digital Marketing

Ads and Headlines

This is the part where you use your writing skills to actually sell the product. There are no subtle hints or hiding behind clever lines. This is advertising designed explicitly to sell.

Ads

The first thing to ask yourself is what is the ad for? If you're running an ad, you want to achieve results that are measurable so that you'll know if your efforts are delivering the desired outcomes. It's really measuring the level of your success and if it hits the milestones.

You are writing an ad because you want people to:
1. Buy your product
2. Hire your company to solve a problem
3. Sign up for a free trial of the product
4. Join a professional organization or association
5. Register for your website
6. Join an event sponsored by your organization
7. Book at your hotel
8. Advertise in your newspaper or online publication
9. Invest in your startup business
10. Send their children to your school
11. Book a flight using your app
12. Order food using your multiplatform app
13. Hire you as a writing consultant

These are just some of the reasons why you're writing an ad. If you notice, they are all measurable; for example, if they buy the product, you can measure the success by looking at the sales numbers.

The point is that you need your ad to sell the product or service you are offering. You're not making an add just to make people become aware of the product. Awareness is hard to measure so it's not a good starting off point when writing an ad.

What do you include in your ad?

1. Benefits of using the product. Let the readers know how the product can solve potential customers' problem. Highlight how it will make things more convenient for the customers if they use the product. The features are great, but what value do they add to make customers' life easier?
2. Answers to any objections or doubts the potential customer may have about the product. How is it different from similar products? Is it more expensive than more recognizable brands?
3. Proof that will support your claims about the product. Prospective buyers want to know if your copy is truthful and effective as advertised.
4. Reassurance through testimonials from customers. Adding endorsements from other companies or influential personalities in the industry will also give your ad some credence.
5. An image or picture. Normally, it's the picture of the product you are trying to sell. However, sometimes people also respond favorably to pictures that show the benefits of the product.
6. A call to action. Those who read your ad already know you're selling a product, so guide them to next step by giving the full details on how to order. If you're selling something else, the call to action would be focused on the desired response or action from your prospective client.

Headlines

Writing a headline is good but writing a headline that converts is even better! This is easier said than done, but it is not impossible to achieve. But first, you must understand why headlines matter.

Headlines do more than just convince your visitors to read your article in its entirety. It can also turn potential leads to actual buying customers. Advertising tycoon David Ogilvy one said that if your headlines don't sell your products, ninety percent of the money invested in advertising and marketing are wasted away.

Headlines are not just sign posts to guide your customers on what to read or where to go, they create first impressions that can keep customers or drive them away. They are that powerful!

From a writing perspective, headlines set the tone for the rest of your article. They act as a gauge on whether your audience will be persuaded to make a purchase or not. If you focus on creating effective headlines, the rest of the work would be easy.

The purpose of the headline is to make people read the first sentence of your article and to keep them reading until they make a purchasing decision.

The Four U's of Headline Writing

- **Unique**

  Don't bother writing headlines if you'll just copy everyone else's headlines. You need headlines that will stand out from a sea of headlines. If people cannot distinguish your headline from that of the competitors, there would be no reason to choose your copy over the others. And this has a direct effect on the product you are writing about. Ultimately, if your headlines don't pull people in, there'll be no interest and no sales.

Never underestimate consumers when it comes to how they view what is being peddled to them. They are more savvy now compared to the consumers of the past. They are put off by blatant marketing tactics that border on misleading the consumers.

They tune out when they hear or read these lines
"But wait, there's more!"
 "If you buy in the next 15 minutes, you'll get not one, not two, but three bottle openers for free!"
"With only three easy payments of $29.99, you can own these leg exercisers today!"

You've all heard these lines before repeatedly. They may have worked splendidly decades ago, but they don't work as much as they did then. Perhaps it works to a certain subset of consumers, but not the majority of consumers. We want to get that bigger piece of the pie and not just the crumbs.

Surely, you can do better than that!

The purpose of your headlines is to make people want to care about your product or service. Studies have shown that 8 out of 10 people will read a great headline, but only 2 out of 10 will read the copy. What this suggests is that people don't care until you give them a reason to care. These are the same people who consume copious amount of media every single day, but most of what they consume are just headlines. Don't think for one minute that they read everything that they see online. Read is too much work for them. Scan is more appropriate. They scan content through headlines.

So, if the headlines are not unique and original, the copies would just be wasted. Being unique means having a personality. If you can inject personality and enthusiasm in your copy, you are more likely to connect with people at a deeper level. Boring has no place in copywriting for web content.
Just ask Gary Vaynerchuk, Neil Patel, Brian Clark, and the people behind Copyblogger and MailChimp. They write the best headlines that draws you to their articles like a moth to a flame. (But please, don't write click-baits. We'll devote a section on discussing this scourge of the internet!)

Here are some examples of unique headlines

"They say the first step is the hardest. So we made it free." MailChimp
"Hello, New York. It's Oscar!"
"This is Who They Call!"
"We're glad you came."
"Start Your Free 30-Day Trial Now"
"Get Started in Less Than 60 Seconds"
"How a Ferrari Made Me A Million Bucks"

- **Ultra-Specific**

Headlines should be more than just specific; it has to be ultra-specific. Interesting details about the product should be presented so that the customers can immediately decide that they want to know more about the product, enough to make them purchase it.

A headline should convey the features and the benefits of the product. One strategy is to single out a specific target. Identify their problem and offer a solution.

For example, if you want to target people who want to earn money in recycling plastics, you must tap into their environmental leanings as well as their entrepreneurial spirit.

"Turn trash into a money-making venture."

You will get their attention because they see the benefit of your offer. When they see "trash" and "money-making" in one sentence, they are hooked. The headline is clear, it's specific, and it's effective. Because it is specific, that target audience are sure to take notice because the headline was particularly targeted at them.

- **Urgency**

Your headline should convey a sense of urgency so that readers would be compelled to continue reading. This does not mean you offer time-sensitive offers. While that works, too, it's a blatant sales pitch that may put off your potential customers.

What it means is that you should make them realize that they could be missing out on something because you are telling them that there is a problem at hand.

When they read the headline, they would be compelled to check out the solution to your problem.

For example:
"Are you losing sales from abandoned carts?"

This headline is targeting e-commerce entrepreneurs and online retailers who are finding that they are losing sales from shopping cart abandonment.

The headline knows the e-tailers' problem of shoppers not completing their purchase and abandoning their shopping cart and the site. So, this piques the interest of the target audience because they want to know what the solution is. It's urgent because they can' afford to keep losing sales.

- **Useful**

Although this is self-explanatory, many marketers and copywriters take this for granted. Among the 4 U's of headline writing, this is the most important. Other elements would not matter if your headline doesn't convey value-added benefits. This is what your customers want. They'll have a greater appreciation of what you're presenting to them if you show them how useful your product is to their business.

Don't fall into the trap of going for clever click-baity headlines thinking that it is the best way to attract customers. Sure, they will be intrigued at the viral headlines, but how about their conversion rates? Probably abysmal.

Clicking on the headlines to read the rest of the article is just the first step of a customer's journey in your website. Your job doesn't end there. You need to guide them through every step of their journey to make sure that they finish the purchase.

Examples of Fantastic Headlines
Become the Best-Dressed Guy in the Room
Create business proposals in minutes
Turn your abandoned carts into 15% more sales
100% Human Transcription Services
They used Pinterest to plan a dream trip
Effortless photo books made with love

Drill #7

Rewrite the following headlines by incorporating the four U's of headline writing.

- Twitter is Still the Fastest Way to Get the News

- The Top Ten Must-Try Restaurants for Millennials

- The App You've Been Saving Up For is Finally Here

Splash/Sales Pages

A splash page is simply a page that appears before any of the pages of your website. It's the first thing visitors see before they are redirected to the main site.

The purpose is to streamline the information that you immediately present to your customers. The information is short and sweet. Users are captive audience of the message because there are no other things to see unless they immediately exit and be redirected to the main website.

There are many ways a splash page can be utilized:

1. It could serve as the welcome page for the website.
2. It could be used to inform visitors of an important update about the company or the site.
3. It could be a teaser that piques the interest of the customer and makes them excited to view the rest of the pages.
4. It could be used as security barrier or a checkpoint of sorts for sites that have mature content. For example, an alcohol site would have a splash page that would check a visitor's age to ensure that they are of the right age.
5. It could be used to ask visitors the language in which they want to view the website in.
6. It could be used to inform visitors that the website experience can be enhanced by turning on the sound.
7. It could be used to inform visitors of fun events like contests and giveaways. It not only livens up the visitor experience, but it also makes them more likely to engage and participate.

Splash pages are used to enhance the site visitors' experience by informing them of updates, news, or anything of value to the visitor.

Two Important Elements of a Splash Page
1. A message
2. An exit button to take the users directly to the website

What to include on a splash page?

- A headline that has a unique value proposition. This proposition is a promise of value that you need to deliver to the customer.
- An eye-catching image that is relevant to the information being provided
- A short write-up (copy) that describes the benefits of the information being presented.
- A Call To Action button
- Trust indicators including customer testimonials and endorsements

Social Media Engagement

Social media can be overwhelming to numerous organizations. Such perception is understandable considering how massive the audience is on every known social media platform. How can businesses even begin to target them, much less engage them?

Is it really possible to have a meaningful social media engagement if the social media landscape has too much noise and too much traffic? The answer lies in a clear understanding of social media engagement.

What is social media engagement?
In technical terms, social media engagement is the measure of how effective your social media efforts are. The articles you publish, the tweets you send, and the posts you make are measured in shares, likes, comments, and other metrics to evaluate the performance of your social media campaigns.

Currently, the three most popular social media sites are:

- ✓ Facebook – engagement with users are through shares, likes, comments, and follows

- ✓ Twitter – engagement with users are through re-tweets, hearts, comments, and follows
- ✓ Instagram – engagement with users are through shares, likes, comments and follows

Shares and likes are gauges of popularity or level of interest. Follows, on the other hand, are indicative of the users wanting to see more of your content on a regular basis. As such, follows have more weight because users can become customers.

In a way, social media engagement is actually the start of nourishing and building a long-term relationship with your audience. As with any relationship, you must be committed to making your customers happy for many years. When you manage to do this, they will reciprocate in the form of customer loyalty.

When customers put their trust into your brand, product, or service to solve their problems, then you are doing something right in the way you manage your social media efforts.

Enhanced Customer Experience
Social media engagement is more than just creating relationships, it's establishing an unforgettable customer experience. The social media platforms enable customers to engage directly with the companies that they support and the brands that they use.

Companies should see this kind of interaction as an opportunity to give them unparalleled service. The conversations in social media are opportunities to win more customers and make old ones stay with you through the long haul.

It's important to respond to customer inquiries in social media in a timely fashion because it means you value the customers' time and effort to reach out to you in a platform of their choosing.

Unfortunately, many companies do not understand the impact of social engagement, that's why messages from customers go unanswered.

There are also cases wherein companies are sold on the idea of using social media but are unprepared and undermanned to respond to a deluge of comments and inquiries. According to studies on social media engagement, customers expect answers from companies within four hours. When this is not fulfilled, it can have a negative impact on companies' reputation on the social media sphere.

Social Media Engagement Best Practices

As with everything else in the realm of social media, there are no hard and fast rules; more so in social media engagement. This is because the dynamics between companies and customers change whenever there is a change in the social media landscape. The engagement strategies that worked before may no longer work now. But experts have found a way to identify the best practices for social media engagement.

✓ **Post content daily**

If you post regularly and consistently, your brand will be on top of the social media newsfeeds. Brand visibility is important to let people know that your products exists. Of course, the content you post must be not only be engaging, but it must also be relevant to your overall social media goals.

Don't overdo your daily postings because people will know that you're only spamming them with your ads. Your posts will be ignored. This impacts your brand reputation negatively, so post a reasonable number of content and interact like a human and not like a spambot.

The safe number is 1 to 3 posts per day. Mix things up by posting a video, an image, and a normal text.

- ✓ **Be personal**
  Don't be a human version of a press release. Let the audience know that you are a real person with a great personality representing your amazing brand. People relate better with brands that have cool people representing them in their social media. Check out Wendy's on Twitter. Be like Wendy's.
- ✓ **Use images and videos**
  Interaction rates to images and videos are sky-high. Research shows that Twitter posts with images increase the likelihood of re-tweets by 35%. Facebook posts with images have an impressive interaction rate, compared to just a measly 4% for text-only posts.
- ✓ **Listen and respond appropriately**
  Engagement is a two-way communication between you and the customer. Hear what people are saying about your product, good or bad. Identify the valid complaints and address them accordingly. Don't ignore the negative criticisms. Respond to them in a professional manner but don't give a canned response.
- ✓ **Contests, giveaways, challenges**
  To drum up interest in your brand or product, you can give away prizes by holding contests. Freebies always increase engagement.

✓ **Collaborate with other popular brands**
Your competitors may not be keen on the idea of collaboration, but brands that are complementary to your brand will most likely take you up on your offer of partnership. Brand advocates are also good candidates for an awesome collaboration.

✓ **Produce content for top social media platforms.**
It's not enough to just post on Facebook. If you limit your presence on one platform, you'll be wasting the opportunity to engage with a massive audience on Twitter, Instagram, and YouTube. You can use one content but tailor-fit it to the platform's format. Image-oriented postings work well on Instagram while videos are better suited on YouTube.

Now that you know the best practices for social media engagement, now learn how to enhance engagement with your audience.

1. Be the conversation starter

If your audience is not responding to regular posts in the way you expect them to, you can initiate the conversation. Sure, they may react lukewarmly, but there's never a guarantee that people will immediately engage on a much deeper level. To improve the conversation, you can do any or all of the following:

✓ Host a Q&A. Schedule the event and build up the excitement. Let them know that they can ask anything about the brand or the product. Don't forget to use a clever hashtag that's a little mysterious just to give them an element of intrigue.

✓ Ask them a question to get the Twitter chat going. React to their answers to keep the chat alive. When people realize that a real person is behind the brand's Twitter account (and not some scheduler that tweets at a designated time), their trust level about the brand will increase.

2. Promote Your Brand Enthusiasts' Content

Brand enthusiasts are people who represent the company's brands in social media. The company sends them products so they can take a picture of them and post them on their various social media accounts.

This works well on Instagram because the images and visuals make the product stand out. What's great about it is the company is promoting a user-generated content. Instead of seeing the product on billboards being used by celebrities, this time, people are seeing the product being used by regular folks. It becomes relatable.

If you want people to participate, you can ask them to post their pics using the product. Use a hashtag to track the performance of the event. You're not only promoting the brand, but you're also showcasing the customers that use your products.

From an analytics standpoint, this kind of engagement will let you see how people are reacting and engaging with the brand. If the brand enthusiasts or social influencers have a massive following, the brand will have greater reach and can potentially get more exposure

3. Jump on Current Events and Trending Topics

Topical events that are trending or going viral are hot topics on social media. You could spark a conversation to bring more traffic to your social networks. For example, if your brand caters to the male demographics, you can create engagement by posting about the NBA playoffs or the NFL Superbowl, or any sporting events. Men love to talk about sports so those who see the posts would be compelled to join the conversation.

You can also use special internet "holidays" like World Pizza Day or World Left-Handed people's Day.

A word of caution though, you have to be sensitive to what you post in relation to the topics or events. There's a thin line that separates a controversial post and a full-on social media disaster. Be aware of the ramifications of an inappropriate promotion.

4. Be Receptive
Social engagement is a two-way street. You can't expect your audience to be fully engaged when you don't respond to their questions in a timely manner.

If you don't respond promptly, your audience will think that you don't value your customers as much as you say you do. Your current customers will abandon you and potential customers will steer clear of the brand.

It may not be obvious at first glance, but the financial ramifications could be a massive blow to the company's bottom line.

Engagement is good, but it's the positive interactions that will make people take notice of your brand. A successful engagement starts when people take in the brand and then it can lead to a conversion. If the customer is happy with the product, they will willingly recommend the product to their friends and followers by posting about their positive experience and writing glowing reviews.

5. Improving Engagement is a Team Effort
Marketing campaigns that focus on improving engagement and increasing the participation of targeted audience have many moving parts, so to speak. It can't be done by a single person. You can't expect the content creators to be the same person to moderate the groups and deal with hostile customers and at the same time serve as an after-sales support representative.

Every brand must have a social media team that consists of:
- ✓ **Content Creators:**
  These people brainstorm, conceptualize ideas, write the script, and produce the content.
- ✓ **Community Managers:**
  These are the regulators in forums, chat groups, or Facebook pages. They handle hostile customers and keep the community as harmonious as it can possibly be. They deal with the internet trolls, the spammers, and those who try to upset the peace and balance. They control the situation when it goes out of hand.
- ✓ **Public Relations:**
  These are the people who know how to give the brand the right exposure using bigger channels. They handle customers, brand partners, collaborators, and the media.

They do damage control when a social media disaster takes place.

✓ **Sales and Enablement:**
These are people who make sure that specific content are given to the people who have shown genuine interest in the brand. The interested parties are usually potential customers who are close to purchasing a product. This groups makes sure that customers complete the purchase.

✓ **Support:**
These are people who monitor that brand's performance and movements in social media. They report their findings to the team and inform them if something needs immediate attention. These people are always ready to put out fires before the situation becomes critical, in the case of a looming social media crisis.

Not all companies have a social media engagement team. Perhaps they do not have the capacity to build one. And that's perfectly fine. What's not okay is when companies have the budget but are not using their resources to improve their social media engagement. This is the reason why questions are left unanswered for days (or if they answered at all) and hostile customers take over the conversation.

Social media engagement is important if a brand wants to get noticed by a massive audience. It's not about going viral or posting clever memes—it's about interacting with the audience and building a relationship that can lead to the achievement of the company's goals.

Content Marketing

Content marketing is a strategy that focuses on creating high-quality relevant content for your target audience with the goal of building a long-term relationship with them.

Essentially, content marketing is about storytelling that gives customers valuable information that will benefit them. Your story is used as a means to attract customers and build a beneficial relationship.

The stories you would be telling can be communicated in many different ways. You can custom-fit your content format based on what your target audience is likely to respond to in a positive manner.

Here is a list of content formats and options that you can use to execute your marketing strategy.

- Blogs
- Case studies
- eBooks
- Emails
- Features
- Guides
- Infographics
- Interviews
- Landing pages
- Lists/Listicles
- News stories
- Press releases
- Research reports
- Slide shows
- Social media posts
- Tutorials

- Videos
- Webinars
- White papers

Content Marketing Strategy
Marketers design a content marketing strategy primarily to engage their audience. Part of the strategy is to track content for lead generation and measure engagement of the company's social media posts.
Before you structure your content marketing campaign, you must first ask yourself the following questions:

✓ Who is your audience?
Think about who you want to reach. Knowing your target audience will give you a crystal-clear idea on what to include in your content.

✓ What channels do you plan to use?
Think about how you will get your message out. Examples of channels you can use are email, search engine ads (e.g. Google Ads), websites, and social media. You can also go the traditional route and create content for print ads, newspapers, pamphlets, and other old-school formats.

✓ What kind of resources do you have?
Before you dive into content creation and marketing campaign, you must do an inventory of what resources you have. Ask yourself these questions:
   - ✓ How many people are in the team?
   - ✓ What skill sets are already available?
   - ✓ What's the marketing budget?
   - ✓ Can the team handle the content creation or should it be outsourced?

Keeping tabs of what your team can and cannot do will help in determining which content can be done immediately and what needs more time to make.

✓ How will you measure the success of your content marketing campaign? What metrics will you be using?

Every you goal you set must be measurable so that you can evaluate the effectiveness of your content marketing efforts. If your marketing campaigns are pushed through social media channels, you can do a social media audit to gauge the success or failure. This way, you can make the necessary adjustments for the next campaign.

✓ What problems (or pain points) are you trying to solve?

Content creation for the sake of posting something on social media does not work most of the time. Everytime you create content, you must have a goal in mind. Think about the pain points of your clients and build your content around providing a solution. Break all the barriers that prevent your client from achieving success.

How to Develop A Content Marketing Strategy
    1. Set your goals and metrics
Set a S.M.A.R.T goal – Specific, Measurable, Attainable, Relevant,

Timely
If your goal is to get more subscribers and viewers for your YouTube video, specify how many subscribers and how many watch hours.

For example, if you want to monetize your channel, you need 1,000 subscribers and 4,000 hours of watch time. That is your goal.

Goals must be measurable, otherwise, you're just wasting your time. For the example above, you can determine if your YouTube campaign works because there are metrics that are used to measure success.

2. Determine the media format to use
The choice of media format would depend on your goal.
If your goal is to entertain:
- ✓ Quizzes
- ✓ Competitions and Contests
- ✓ Games
- ✓ Branded videos
- ✓ Viral videos

If your goal is to educate:
- ✓ Infographics
- ✓ Trend Reports
- ✓ eBooks
- ✓ Articles
- ✓ Demo videos

If your goal is to inspire:
- ✓ Reviews
- ✓ Testimonials
- ✓ Case Studies
- ✓ Celebrity Endorsements

If your goal is to convince:
- ✓ Product Features and Benefits
- ✓ Interactive Demos
- ✓ Product Ratings and Reviews
- ✓ Testimonials

✓ Data Sheet
✓ Product Comparison

3. Conduct a Content Audit

A content audit will help you identify what's working for the brand and what's not. By auditing your content, you'll identify which social media channels and media formats are effective in communicating your message across. You'll be able to pinpoint the content that your target audience is most receptive to.

If your content marketing campaign is online-centric, then pushing them through social media channels is a smart decision. However, it doesn't stop there. Performing a social media audit is beneficial because you'll see what types of content performed well. They can be duplicated so that success can be duplicated as well.

4. Map a customer journey

Content marketing is essentially mapping a customer's journey from being a target audience to being a lead to being a prospective buyer to being a purchasing customer.

Given that it takes time to convert a target audience to a paying customer, your content must be designed to follow this journey.

Marketing can be implemented in stages or phases:
1. Phase 1: Creating Awareness
This is the phase where your goal is to attract the right audience.
Content examples: articles, blog posts, infographics, podcasts, tip sheets, eBooks, assessments, webinars

2. Phase 2: Building Up Interest

This is the phase where you turn prospects into leads. Content examples: training videos, solution videos, virtual events, worksheets, presentations

3. Phase 3: Consideration.
This is the phase where customers strongly consider your brand as a preference over others.
Content examples: data sheets, buying guide, product features, and benefits, case studies, free trials, testimonials, reviews, ratings

4. Phase 4: Decision and Conversion
This is the phase where a lead is converted to a paying customer.

5. Phase 5: Service and Support
This is the phase where you follow through the sales by providing customer service and support. You continue to create content that will help the customers to understand how the product works so that it will solve their problems.
When a company does a good job in guiding the customers in their purchasing journey, brand loyalty is established.

Email Marketing

Email marketing is a strategy wherein products and services are promoted using email as the platform. As the approach becomes more sophisticated over the years, email marketing evolved and became a tool to develop relationships with potential customers and clients.

The approach is essentially the modern version of direct mail marketing, with the only difference is that instead of sending materials through the postal service, they are sent electronically through email.

Even with the rise of social media platforms, email marking continues to be the weapon of choice of marketers. Why? Because it generates the highest return on investment (ROI) for marketers.

This may be surprising to marketers who abandoned all email marketing hope and switched to the more flamboyant social media counterparts. Clearly, that's a bad decision because email marketing generates more ROI than any other online platform. In fact, for every $1 spent on email marketing, it generates $38 in ROI.

If that is not enough reason to convince you to get back to email marketing, these 7 email marketing facts should do the trick:

1. **Larger reach**

   Don't be blinded by astronomical number of users of Facebook (2.32 billion), YouTube (1.3 billion), Twitter (326 million monthly users), and Instagram (1 billion) because they're mostly for online socialization. Unless a company really designs its marketing campaigns around these platforms, they got nothing on email marketing when it comes to effective way of reaching out to various audiences.

While social media has impressive numbers, email reigns supreme. According to a study by Radicati Group, it is projected that the number of email users will reach more than 3.8 billion by the start of 2019. This should not come as a surprise because all you have to do is look at your online behavior. Everything you do online requires an email address—create a social media account, purchase items, sign up for newsletters, or make any transaction.

Anybody who's online has an active email address even if they do not have social media account. In that sense, email is the supreme currency of the web. In terms of connecting with prospective customers and clients, there's no other channel that has a wider reach than email.

2. Email delivers your message 90% of the time.

You might think that 10% is a lot of undelivered emails, so how does that make email better than, say, Facebook?

When you send a message to your intended recipient, it gets delivered no matter what. While on Facebook, only 2% of your fans will see your posts because Facebook limits the appearance of your posts in the News Feed. The reason for this is to drive companies to avail of paid advertising.

To illustrate, if you post an update to your 20,000 fans, only 400 fans will have the chance to see it—and that is if your post doesn't get buried in a sea of posts from families, friends, and other pages.

When you send an email to your subscribers, it means they willingly signed up for your mailing list because they want to hear from you.

So, between fans who may or may not see your posts and fans who explicitly want to get updates from you, you'll have better chances with the latter.

3. Email drives sales conversions

In marketing, the end goal is to turn prospective customers into paying customers. It has always been this way for a very long time, but the marketing methods have changed dramatically with the rise of online platforms.

The people in your mailing list are potential customers that have already heard of your product. Signing up to your mailing list or newsletter means they are interested in what you have to offer. By giving you their emails, they are allowing you to send them updates.

So, if you send them an email with a link to your sales page, they're most likely click on it. The strategy does not work as well with social media platforms. For example, if you put your website URL in a Twitter post, those who see your post will not click on it unless they are interested in what you have to say. So your marketing efforts will end with fewer conversions.

Whereas with email, the click-through rate is about 3% of the total recipient. That's not too bad compared to Twitter's 0.5% click-through rate.

4. Email is (still) the preferred communication medium

More and more people are now communicating and reaching out to audiences through various social media channels. But the type of communication is informal and casual. People are there to look at photos, watch videos, and read posts. However, when it comes to business transactions, email is preferred because it is more professional.

When customers buy products, they expect to get updates on their emails. When they have a complaint, they send email to the company. When they want more details about a product, they want it sent to their emails.

Email is still the more reliable communication channel compared to social media. That's why marketers can't and won't quit it.

5. Email is not controlled or limited by any entity

Unlike Facebook who controls the content that people see on their news feed, email is not restricted by any one particular entity. If you send an email, it will be delivered to the intended recipients without censure.

If you invest time and money in building a mailing list, it will be an asset that you can use to grow your brand. There is no one there to stop you or threaten to stop you.

6. Email is forever

Social media platforms come and go (R.I.P. MySpace, Friendster, Google+) but email is forever. Users are fickle. When something that is perceived to be better, they will jump ship. MySpace was once the largest social network platform from 2005-2008. It even surpassed

Google as the most visited website in the United States in 2006. It was so huge that you'd think it wouldn't fail, and yet it did. So, imagine if you have designed your marketing campaign around that platform to build an audience only to find it dead as a doornail a year later. That would a marketing catastrophe of biblical proportions.

On the other hand, email is still standing and stronger than ever. When it comes to platform stability, an email list is much more stable than a social media following.

Email Marketing Tips to Get You Started

1. Build Your Own List

Building a mailing list takes time. It's so challenging that enterprising people are building lists and selling them to companies who are willing to pay big money for such a precious commodity.

The truth is that doing so is just a waste of time and money. First of all, you don't know how they got the list. They could have acquired it through illegal means and you wouldn't know any better. Secondly, the people on the list may not be your target audience. Sending them emails would be useless. Worse, they would even flag your emails as spam.

You can grow your mailing list by giving visitors of your website or blog something that is of value to them in exchange for their sign up or subscription to your newsletter. You can give them a free eBook, free consultation, trial offers, vouchers, or any other sweeteners.

2. Build a rapport with people in your list

Although your intention is to sell, don't overdo it. Use your list to build a relationship with your customers or potential customers. Share expertise, tips, insights, or anything of value to them. In the process, they are getting to know more about the product or the brand.

3. Follow the rules of CAM-SPAM Act

Make sure that you are not violating any rules of the said Act. You should not be deceptive in you subject line. Some marketers deceive their own customers by saying something is free, but in truth, they have to make a purchase first to avail of the freebie.

You should also provide a method of unsubscribing to the mailing list or newsletter. This way, those who signed wouldn't feel that they are trapped in a place they don't want to be in.

At the end of every email, you should indicate a name and address of the contact person of the company. This shows that your company is transparent and has nothing to hide.

4. Stick to a schedule when sending out newsletters.

Newsletters are not meant to be sent daily. The content is mostly a summary of events that happened for a particular period of time. It also has announcements and other important information. It's good practice to follow a regular schedule so that the customers know when to expect your newsletter.

Emails that Make You Click

Just how does your email stand out in an over-crowded inbox? People receive tons of emails on a daily basis. You can't assume that you're the only mailing list that your target customers have signed for.

They've probably signed up for your competitors' newsletters as well.
With all the offers and notifications that they receive every single day, how can you make them notice you?

Here are some best practices on how you can get your recipients to open, read, and click on your email:

- **Choose your email's subject line wisely**

Your subject can make or break your email marketing campaign. It has to make a great first impression, otherwise, it will go unread or worse, sent to the spam folder.

Just like a headline, the subject must be direct to the point. Avoid buzz words, jargons, and spammy words. Spam filters are much more sophisticated now so if you're not smart about the words you use, your subject can trigger spam filters.

Avoid clickbait at all cost. Clickbaits are more focused on clicks rather than conversion. Most of them have nothing to do with the content of the email.

- **Formulas trump templates**

You might be compelled to use email templates because you need a quick email content. While that's an acceptable practice, you are forced to adhere to a certain format. Your email will not stand out if it's just more of the same.

Remember AIDA and PAS? Those are formulas you can count on, especially in email copywriting. They make your writing more fluid and they allow you to actually be creative. You can tailor-fit your message to your specific audience.

- **Be personal**

Write as if you're talking to just one person. It makes your recipient feel special because you give the impression that you've spent time to craft an email specifically for that person. Use the You Language to give your email the personal touch. As they say, if you write to everyone, you write to no one.

It's a plus if you address the recipient by their name and the sender's name is used instead of just the company name or the marketing department.

- **Keep it concise**

Email is a flexible medium that it's easy to tailor-fit your message to your target audience. It's a double-edged sword because since it's flexible, you may be tempted to ramble and go off at a tangent.

Stick to the point of the message, which is to provide a solution to a customer's problem. There's no room for irrelevant narratives.

- **Repeat your call to action**

A call to action can appear at any part of your email. Many businesses make the mistake if saving it for the last. Don't hesitate to repeat your call to action because customers need to be guided in their purchasing journey.

Drill #8

Study the following (real) email subject lines and write the body of the email.

1. "Uh-oh, your prescription is expiring" (Sender: Warby Parker)

2. "The timer's going off on your cart!" (Sender: King Arthur Flour)

3. "What Did You Think? Write a Review" (Sender: REI)

4. "Rock the color of the year" (Sender: Etsy)

5. "DO NOT Commit These Instagram Atrocities (Sender: Thrillist)

Google Ads

Although Google is the most popular and widely used search engine in the world, it has more functions than just crawling the web for keywords. Google also offers advertisements to those who need them. These ads appear on top of the search engine results page (SERP) before the actual results of a specific keyword search or organic links.

What are Ads and AdSense and why should you care?
Google's advertisements are coursed through its AdWords and AdSense programs. When you avail of these services, your ads would appear as "sponsored results" or "sponsored ads" on Google's page.

Google Ads (formerly Google AdWords) is a complex auction system of sorts that focus on keywords. Advertisers can choose from a list of keywords to target. These keywords must be related to their brand or product offering. Simply put, these are words that people are most likely to search on Google.

As it is an auction system, advertisers bid on these highly sought keywords. Each bid is based on how much they want to pay for a Google user to click on their ad. Google assigns a Quality Score based on the quality of the proposed ad. The bid and the Quality Score will determine which Google ads appear on the SERP.

Every user click, the advertiser pays the calculated cost per click. If you "win" the AdWords auction, your ads will appear for relevant keywords. But before you can win, you'll have to optimize your Quality Score and bid amount. These two elements are necessary to determine your ad positioning. Needless to say, a high Quality Score will give you a better ad positioning on the Google search page giving your ad higher exposure and lower cost per click, which improves your ROI.

It may be difficult to understand if you are new to Google Ads, but if you understand how keywords work, you're good to go.

How to write a Google Ad?

Right off the bat, a Google Ad is extremely challenging because you are only given 30 characters for the headline and 80 characters for the description. These are the limits that you have to work with. These are even shorter than Twitter's maximum character count of 280.

So, here are some tips in creating an effective and Google-friendly ad:

1. **Cut all the fluff:** Choose your words wisely and make every word count. There's no room for long headlines and flowery descriptions. Get to the point.
2. **Mirror your prospective customer's end goal:** This is the part where you tell people that you are giving them a solution to your problem in 30 characters or less.

Drill #9

Here's an example of simple yet effective Google ad:
   New Nutella Pancake Recipes
   nutsaboutpancakes.com/NutellaPancakeRecipes
   Faster way to wake the kids up in the morning.
   Want it? Download Now!

It has a headline, keyword, benefit, and call to action.

Now, create a Google Ad using the features and benefits of the soon-to-be-launched tablet discussed in Chapter 1.

Chapter 6 Scribe Support

Breaking Writer's Block

Writer's block is real, whether you believe it or not. It's something that's bound to happen at some point in a writer's life. When it hits, it feels like every writing moment is an uphill climb. You're battling with the writing demons and guess who's winning? Not you.

What is Writer's Block?

A fairly accurate description is that writer's block is a psychological inhibition that prevent a person from starting or completing a piece of writing. Based on this definition, writer's block is all in the mind.

Not all psychologists subscribe to the idea that writer's block is a psychological condition. Writer and psychologist Susan Reynolds explains that writing is a mental process that involves "hardcore, cognitive expenditure". Writers tend to struggle because they are simply mentally drained and not because they are psychologically inhibited.

Whether writer's block is a myth or psychological inhibition is no longer a contention when the condition rears its ugly head.

Reasons for Writer's Block

- **Fear**

Many writers are overcome with fear. They fear that their work would be criticized by people. They fear that the publishers would reject their manuscripts. And above all, they fear that they are not cut out to be a writer. So, instead of putting themselves and their bodies of work out there, they'd rather do something else. The fear of failing made them resist what they want to do in the first place.

- **Self-Doubt and Self-Criticism**

You are your own worst critic. The more you criticize your work, the more your self-doubt is magnified. What's worse, you compare your work with that of others who are more successful than you are. If you constantly do this, you are belittling yourself, your capabilities, and your achievements as a writer. You are unfairly criticizing yourself. When you lose confidence in your writing, then it would be difficult to get into your writing groove. And when you finally get to writing, you'll think that nothing you create would ever be good enough.

- **Perfectionism**

There's nothing wrong in wanting to achieve perfection when it comes to your craft. However, in your quest for perfection, you put undue pressure on yourself. You try to prevent criticisms from getting to you so your solution is to write the perfect sentences to make perfect paragraphs that would ultimately make the perfect novel. You have to remember that it is not realistic to think that everyone would love your work. It just doesn't work that way. People will always find something to criticize about no matter how great the work is.

- **Resistance**

In the book The War of Art, author Steven Pressfield talked about an internal force that stops people from finishing their creative endeavors. He calls it resistance. You can easily recognize this when it's taking you forever to do something that can normally done in just a few minutes. Or when you'd rather do something else which is a whole lot easier to do than the thing that you should be doing. That is resistance. You resist because the mixture of fear, pressure, and stress is gnawing at you, preventing to complete what you have started. Your resistance is a defense mechanism. You somehow take comfort in that because you can't deal with the negative criticisms when your put your work out there for people to see and scrutinize.

How to Overcome Writer's Block

1. Save something for the next writing session

Writers can write on the fly and when pressured to do so by publishers, authors, or bosses. Oftentimes, when there is a small window of time to complete the work, you give it all you've got just to make the deadline. The problem is you've used up all your resources and you've got nothing left to write. You're just drawing blanks.

When you are in the writing zone, you are invincible! You keep going and going until you finish your writing project. Instead of doing that, stop mid-way through when you still have all these great ideas in your mind. You don't want to use all your resources in just one project. Pace yourself so that in your next writing session, you'll have something you can start with.

2. Write Daily

Make writing a daily habit. You can start small or start slow. It doesn't matter what you write, just write something every single day.

When something becomes a habit, it becomes second nature. When you write on a daily basis, everything becomes automatic. You don't have to think about doing it anymore because it's already internally programmed and ready to go. The great thing about this is that there's no more room for stress and fear to slither their way into your mind.

3. Reinforce Your Writing Habit

It's easy to "cheat" on a daily writing habit challenge because you can always say that you would do more writing tomorrow to make up for the days you didn't do any writing. The problem here is the more you avoid writing, the more writing you need to do to catch up. That just defeats the purpose of the exercise.

To avoid a writing disaster, you must track your progress (or non-progress). The best way to do this is to have a writing calendar. All you have to do is to mark your calendar with an "X" for every day you complete a writing session.

This is called the "Seinfeld Method". Jerry Seinfeld, as you probably know, is one of the most prolific writers in the entertainment industry. He wrote better jokes because he wrote every single day. When he was just starting his career as a comedian, he would have a wall calendar that has the entire year on one page. He would hang it prominently on a wall. For each day he completed a writing task, he would be a big red "X" over that day. As he kept doing it, he built a chain of Xs. One of the motivations is to NOT break that chain. You can replicate this method if you are up to the challenge.

Make it easy for you to do this by putting a huge calendar on your desk or in the bathroom (any place you go to repeatedly every single day). The point of this exercise is to reinforce your writing habit. The more you write, the better you become at doing it. It is the consistent daily writing that will help you achieve extraordinary outcomes.

4. Brainstorm

The power of brainstorming is discussed in detail in Chapter 3. Brainstorming is effective creating ideas and ideas especially if you're stuck in a rut. In writing, brainstorming can be done in different ways:

- ✓ **Freewriting**
  Write down anything that comes to your mind within a 5-minute time limit. Let the ideas flow through writing and don't edit yourself. The exercise is not concerned about structure or relevance. It is simply trying to get you in the state of creative thinking.
- ✓ **Use Writing Prompts**
  Prompts relieve you of the pressure of coming up with clever ideas. They are ready-made questions or phrases that you just have to answer or complete. They are a great way to start writing. Once you get into the writing groove, you'll find that ideas will start to come out.
- ✓ **Think Like A Journalist**
  If you are working on a topic and you don't know how to begin writing, ask yourself the Who? When? Where? When? Why? and How? of your topic. This would allow you to think of the topic at various angles. It gives you a lot more options and you can build up from there.
- ✓ **Idea Mapping or Clustering**

From a general idea, you can extract sub-ideas. This is an exercise that lets your mind think of connections. The more connections you think of, the higher the chance of narrowing down your topics until you get to the topic that you are excited to write about.

✓ **Fill in the Blanks**
Using the "X is Y" approach will force you to think of correlations, connections, and causations. This way, you'll find a different perspective when you are finding it hard to expound on a particular topic.

For example: _____ is/was/are/were_____
Topic: Writer's Block
       Writer's block is stopping me from completing my ad copy.
The delay in submitting the copy is delaying the launch of the marketing campaign

5. Switch to Another Activity
Sometimes, when you step away from the task, you are able take your mind off the pressure and the stress. Do something else like exercise, go shopping, take a walk, walk the dog, cook a nice meal—anything that is remotely related to writing. It could be other creative outlets or just a random activity. It's a way to reboot yourself to flush out the pressure of writing.

A Dose of Inspiration
Even famous writers and bestselling authors experience writer's block. They struggled with it perhaps more often than they let show, but they found ways to overcome it. Some of the best writing came after a serious bout of writer's block. Here are

some authors who beat writer's block and the strategies they used to reawaken their writing mojos.

- ✓ Maya Angelou: Keep writing even if you are not pleased with the outcome. Do not overthink.
- ✓ Neil Gaiman: Put your writing aside for a few days. This is what he calls his hibernation strategy. Doing other things for a while so that when you get back to writing, you feel all the excitement coming back as if you're doing it for the first time.
- ✓ Anthony Trollope: Set a daily word count goal. This is part of his "timed writing" strategy. It doesn't matter if it's long or short, as long as you write at a specific time frame. Trollope wrote 250 words every 25 minutes.
- ✓ Toni Morrison: Have a writing ritual. She emphasized that performing a pre-writing ritual helps you mentally prepare for the actual writing. It helps to get you into that space where you are at your best.
- ✓ Ernest Hemingway: Maintain your writing momentum by not using all your resources in one sitting. Don't use all your ideas and energy in one writing session so that you still have something left for the day after and the next.

Writer's block is just a temporary obstacle to your writing. It can be discouraging and dispiriting, but it's not something you can't fix. It can be beaten with the right approach and attitude. It's just a minor hiccup in your writing process. Identify what's causing your writer's block so that you can find effective way to overcome it. Giving up is not an option.

Drill #10

Destroy writer's block with these creative writing prompts specifically designed for copywriting.

1. Think of 3 song titles and use it to promote a product.
2. Write a headline to convince a friend that she needs a product that she does not normally use.
3. Write a Google Ad for the last item you purchased online.

Time Management Hacks

Time is an important commodity for writers. Because there is a massive demand for fresh content daily, writers become content factories that produce an insane amount of materials that cover virtually every topic known to mankind. There is a great pressure meet the demand but there seems to be not enough time in the day to do everything.

If you find yourself struggling to meet your deadlines and losing sleep about it, then you are failing miserably at time management. It does not help that there are so many distractions that slow you down like social media and Netflix.

If you are stuck in a time loop where all you do is work, sleep and not much else, you need a time management intervention. If you master time management, you'll be more productive and finish your work ahead of the deadline with lots of time to spend in things that matters most.

There is no one-size-fits-all time management solution, so here are time management hacks that you can implement in your life so that you can become a more productive writer with more time in your hands.

- **Create a To-Do List**

If you are overwhelmed by the number of tasks that you have to accomplish in a day, you need to organize them and list them down by level of priority or urgency. Time-sensitive tasks are on top of the list followed by tasks that do not have specific deadlines but needs to be done within the day. If you follow your To-Do list for the day, you are taking away the unnecessary stress of thinking about things that are not on the list. Crossing off items on your list is one of the best feelings in the world. It gives you a satisfying feeling that you have accomplished something.

- **Plan Your Day**

When you wake up in the morning, create a schedule of the things that you will be doing for the entire day. This gives you control of how your day would go. It also gives you the opportunity to identify the things that you do which can be categorized as "time-wasters". There's no harm in indulging in some of that, but if you have a schedule, you will be setting your unproductive activities to a minimum.

- **Pomodoro Technique**

This technique was created by Frances Cirillo which breaks down the task or work into intervals. A 25-minute work is followed by a 3-5-minute break. You will have to do this four times.

After clocking in four (4) 25-minute period, you can then take a 15-30-minute break, after which you start all over again until you complete your work. The short breaks in between work are important for the body to relax and recharge when your productivity level plateaus. You'll find that you would be more productive once you have those mini-breaks instead of working for hours straight.

- **Start Your Day Earlier**

When you wake up before everyone else, you can have that moment of peace and quiet to do simple things without distraction. That "extra" time can be used to check and respond to emails or start with your writing rituals. So that by the time chaos ensues, you have already done something productive and you don't have to think about them anymore. You can focus on other tasks.

- **Turn off Notifications**

How many times in a day does your phone alert you with notifications from email and other apps? Too many! The problem with notifications is that they disrupt your work as well as your concentration. When you hear the notification sound, you feel that you need to respond to it because it gives you a false sense of urgency. You bounce between thoughts and tasks which makes you lose focus on the important task.

Of course, this doesn't mean that you don't check your emails. You still have to respond to them in a timely manner. What you have to do is to set a specific time for checking of emails and social media.

- **Stop Multitasking**

Contrary to popular belief, multitasking is not an effective way to work or produce results. It is wasteful and inefficient because the time you spend jugging several tasks could have been used to focus on finishing a single task.

Multitasking only gives the false impression that you are busy. But keep in mind that being busy is not the same thing as being productive. You can get more done by prioritizing a task instead of doing several tasks at the same time. You can allocate time in the morning to work on the urgent tasks and then allow yourself to take a break before moving on to the next priority task.

- **Complete an easier task before moving on to the toughest ones.**

The reason behind this is that it will made you feel good by getting easy wins right off the bat. It gives you momentum and drive to take on the more difficult tasks of the day. This works because when you accomplish something early in the day, it gives you an extra boost of confidence to take on the bigger tasks.

- **Declutter and organize your workspace**

Renowned organizing consultant Marie Kondo advocates for cleaning and tidying up your workspace. Clutter is chaos. If your desk is littered with papers, trinkets, cords, cable, Post-it notes, take-out wrappers, crumbs, food scraps, and dead bugs, you need to declutter fast!

It may not be obvious to you, but the clutter on your desk adds to your stress. It takes your attention away from your work. It signals the brain that your task is not done because you're seeing all the mess and that things are not in their proper places.

Prevent your workspace from becoming a disaster area by cleaning the mess frequently. Do a little purging on regular basis and get rid of items that you don't really need. Items that don't add to your productivity must be put away. After you have used the items, put them back to where they belong. If items are in their proper places, you wouldn't waste time searching for them.

- **Learn How to say "No"**

There will be bosses, colleagues, friends, family members, or pets who will demand your attention and invade your time. If you're on the clock and you allow them to interrupt you, they're taking precious time off your work. It disrupts what you're doing and it delays your work process.

There are also people who would come to you for help even if they are capable of finding solutions to their problems. Let them know that you cannot accommodate their request because you are on the clock. By saying "no", you are preventing these "time vampires" to suck time out of your workday. You must draw the line.

- **Learn shortcuts**

There are many productivity tools that can automate processes and make your life easier. Many of these tools are apps that you can use with your phones or mobile devices. Even in using spreadsheets and word processors, there are shortcuts you can use to cut the process time in half. If you apply that to your everyday work, you will see that
your productivity will rise with half the effort.

- **Delegate Tasks and Outsource Processes**

The reality is that you can't do everything on your own if you are pressed for time. There are certain tasks that you can delegate to other members of your team. Just make sure that the person you choose is highly skilled and reliable. It will be difficult to do this initially because in your mind, you're the best person to complete the task. However, if you spread the work, you and your team can finish the task in less time.

If you work alone, you can outsource the task. Just make sure you do your research and due diligence to ensure that you are hiring the right kind of people for the task.

- **Set Deadlines**

A deadline is a motivation for people to start working. Knowing the deadline means you can schedule your entire day around that deadline. It's a great way to keep track of your progress. You'll know when you're getting behind the schedule or on track to completion. Without a deadline, you are more likely to procrastinate.

Editing Tips

So, you've finished writing your copy! Congratulations are in order. You may have aced the writing process, but you still need to tighten your copy. First drafts are always crappy, so you need to make some adjustments. You might say that you have editors for that kind of work and you are right.

However, not everyone can afford editors, so self-editing is the usual route in this case. But even if you have an editor, there's no harm in reviewing your copy. That way, you can focus on tightening up your sentences and get rid of major flaws, unnecessary words, and glaring errors.

Tips in Revising and Tightening Your Copy

- ### Break up long sentences

Long sentences have no place in a copy because they come across as confusing and boring. They are harder to understand and may put off the readers. Long sentences usually contain several ideas so instead of cram them in one sentence, cut them into two or break them into shorter sentences.

- ### Ditch the adverbs

Adverbs are excess words, therefore, unnecessary in a copy. They don't add value to the copy because you're just using a weak verb and adding the suffix "-ly".

To illustrate:
1. *The cat walks slowly.*
2. *The cat tiptoes.*

Sentence #2 is more descriptive and reads better.

- ### Use the active voice

Writing sentences in active voice means that the subject performs the action denotes by the verb. Passive voice, on the other hand, the subject of the sentences is being acted upon.

Using active voice makes your sentences straightforward. They paint a clear image of what you are trying to convey to the readers.

- ### Eliminate extra punctuation

Hyphens and semicolon are effective in proving a point, but if your writing is littered with these types of punctuation, they affect the flow of your sentences.

You can remove the extra punctuation by restructuring the sentences or ending the sentence and starting a new one to introduce a separate idea.

- **Use words that people are familiar with**

Don't use jargons because not everyone understands them. Stuffy words don't make your writing sound intelligent; they make your writing sound pretentious and unrelatable.

- **Use stronger verbs**

Stronger verbs have more impact to the readers. They create a detailed image in the reader's mind of what you're trying to convey.

For example:
"make your copy stronger"
"strengthen your copy"

In these two examples, the word "strengthen" is stronger than "to make"

Tips in Self-Editing Your Copy

Editing can transform a mediocre piece of writing into a great content. Whether you have a professional editor or not, it is important to self-edit your work. By doing so, you can catch errors and bad structure so that you can make the necessary corrections.

- **Read your work out loud:**
  This allows you to hear the rhythm of your writing. If something is off, you will hear it. Poorly worded sentences do not flow together.
- **Read your work in a different format:**
  Try switching font styles or even sizes.

- **Use Text-to-Speech platform:**
  If no one is available to read your copy to you, use online text-to-speech software or app to listen to your work. When words are mispronounced, they're more likely spelled incorrectly.
- **Remove word that denotes uncertainty:**
  When you're writing to persuade readers, your copy must sound authoritative and firm. Refrain from using phrases like "seems to be", might be", or "looks like". Your copy will sound indecisive and weak.
- **Avoid repetitive phrases:**
  If you use the same phrases to make a point, your copy would sound like a broken record. Use a variety of phrases that mean the same thing but would not sound repetitive. Find alternatives by consulting a thesaurus.
- **Use a proofreading software:**
  MS Word has a built-in spellchecker and grammar checker you can use to proofread your work. There are also third-party software you can use to spot spelling and grammar mistakes. These programs cover advanced grammar rules that may not be available in your word processing programs. Consult a reputable writing manual when you are unsure about the writing style, word usage, and sentence construction.

Conclusion

Congratulations! You've unlocked Copywriting Level: Master Manipulator.

You're now armed with the skills and tools to create content that not only inform customers, but also persuade them to take a specific action. As a copywriter, you're not just feeding customers high-quality and valuable content, you are also giving them a real solution to their specific problems.

Words will be extremely powerful when used right. Through words, you have the power to connect with your target audience. You can guide them in their customer journey from start to finish.

The principles of copywriting are still the same. You still have to understand your target audience and figure out their needs, wants, and pain points. You still have to trigger all sorts of emotions to compel them to pay attention and take action. You still have to persuade them that your product is the best choice among hundreds of products in the market. But this time, it's all digital.

Copywriting has evolved. Messages are now being delivered to the intended audiences at a breakneck speed. With various social media platforms, content are consumed faster. As a result, more content are created every single minute.

With the lessons you've learned from this guidebook, you can rise to the challenges of copywriting in the digital age.

You got this!

Please keep in touch with me and updated with me at:

https://wswainbrand.com/

Thanks for Reading!

What did you think of, **Killer Copywriting Revolution: Master The Art Of Writing Copy That Sells (Two Book Bundle)**

I know you could have picked any number of books to read, but you picked this book and for that I am extremely grateful.

I hope that it added at value and quality to your everyday life. If so, it would be really nice if you could share this book with your friends and family by posting to Facebook and Twitter.

If you enjoyed this book and found some benefit in reading this, I'd like to hear from you and hope that you could take some time to post a review. Your feedback and support will help this author to greatly improve his writing craft for future projects and make this book even better.

I want you, the reader, to know that your review is very important and so, if you'd like to leave a review, all you have to do is click here and away you go. I wish you all the best in your future success!

Please keep in touch with me and updated with me at:

https://wswainbrand.com/

Thank you and good luck!

William Swain

Claim This Now

The Ultimate Guide to Make Money Onlines

Grab your chance to own this comprehensive two audiobook bundle by Max Lane, covering everything you need to know about how to make money online and passive income ideas.

Including:

- *Make Money Online: Twelve Proven Methods to Earn Passive Income and Work from Anywhere in the World*
- *The Fastlane to Make Money Online: How to Write a Book and Make Passive Income with Self Publishing, Audiobooks and More*

Do you want to learn how to make money online consistently? Without a lot of fuss, scams, or investing any money?

If so - you've come to the right place....

THE ULTIMATE GUIDE TO MAKE MONEY ONLINE

Build a Passive Income Fortune with Kindle Publishing, Amazon FBA, Affiliate Marketing, Dropshipping, YouTube, Udemy, Blogging, Shopify and much more

(TWO BOOK BUNDLE)

FREE! Report reveals our most popular article headlines for driving traffic and attracting readers!

Find Out More

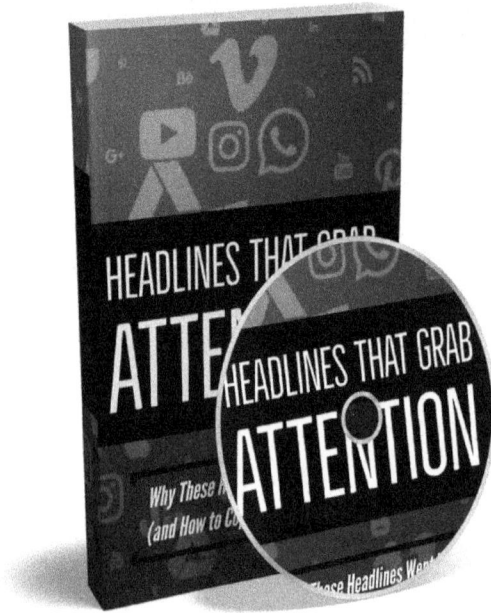